"*Letters from Home* is a creative, inspirational and hopeful book for any parent who wants to inspire their child to live a successful life. It empowers parents to wisely influence and educate their children about how to meaningfully navigate the challenging journey called life, so that they can become the moral person, passionate professional and altruistic member of society, they were always meant to be. David and Andrea Reiser cleverly weave wise and personal letters about life to their four children, and mix them with a little bit of history and other compelling stories to further highlight these essential and classic messages, which too often get lost in today's morally confused society. Bravo!! And thank you for writing this jewel of a book, for all of us to treasure."

—Robi Ludwig, Psy.D.
NBC *Today* show contributor

"America is the 'land of opportunity'—not through a pre-ordained right, but through hard work, integrity, and vision. In our increasingly global economy, *Letters from Home* reminds us of the principles that make America great today, and that our children will need tomorrow. Wisdom for all ages leaps off the pages, as *Letters from Home* brings the American spirit to life for the whole family."

—Mark Palmer
CEO, StreamBase Systems

"*Letters from Home* is a beautiful reminder that true success means much more than money and materialism. It means embracing the responsibility of giving back to others with your hands and your heart: from the planet itself to the brotherhood and sisterhood of humanity to the local community to the small cadre of friends and loved ones we call family. If all young Americans took inspiration from the lessons in this book, together we'd create the kind of world we all wish for."

—Andy Sabin
President, Andrew Sabin Family Foundation

"Letters from Home poignantly outlines the building blocks we need to teach our children—and sometimes, each other—about what it means to be good citizens of the world. This is not simply a book about how one achieves success in life; it is about the importance of family, respect, integrity, work ethic, and determination on life's journey—factors easily lost or forgotten in today's fast paced, smart phone-crazed world. Through letters to their four sons and profiles of their friends and acquaintances, David and Andrea Reiser give us unique glimpses into the way in which they and others in their community have realized their dreams, and remind us that the true definition of success in life has little to do with money, and more to do with what we give back to this world."

—Sheila Lirio Marcelo
Founder & CEO, Care.com

"In *Letters from Home* David and Andrea Reiser lay out for their four sons the structure within which they have been raised—a structure that stresses honesty, decency and a path to success in life that is based on traditional American values. It is a timely message for these young men as they move into manhood. It is a timeless message that they can pass on to their children and grandchildren."

—Geraldine A. Ferraro

"David and Andrea Reiser in *Letters from Home* create a prescription for happiness, prosperity and fulfillment in life that works for everybody—traditional virtues and values to guide young Americans as well as corporate CEOs. In an era where many Americans believe we have lost our compass, this book shares a playbook that inspires us to make the world a better place and to work hard to achieve the American Dream for ourselves and our families. Their passion for a meaningful and good life is deliciously contagious and worth passing on to all whom you love."

—Howie Phanstiel
Retired Chairman & CEO, PacifiCare Health Systems

LETTERS

—◄ *from* ►—

HOME

A WAKE-UP CALL FOR SUCCESS & WEALTH

DAVID R. REISER AND ANDREA R. REISER

WILEY

John Wiley & Sons, Inc.

Published by John Wiley & Sons, Inc., Hoboken, New Jersey.
Published simultaneously in Canada.

For general information on our other products and services or for technical support, please contact our Customer Care Department within the United States at (800) 762-2974, outside the United States at (317) 572-3993 or fax (317) 572-4002.

Wiley also publishes its books in a variety of electronic formats. Some content that appears in print may not be available in electronic books. For more information about Wiley products, visit our web site at www.wiley.com.

Library of Congress Cataloging-in-Publication Data:

Reiser, David R.
    Letters from home : a wake-up call for success and wealth / David R. Reiser, Andrea Reiser.
        p.   cm.
    Includes index.
    ISBN 978-0-470-63792-0 (cloth); 978-0-470-92883-7 (ebk); 978-0470-92884-4 (ebk)
    1. Success in business—Case studies.   2. Businesspeople—Conduct of life—Case studies.   3. Success.   4. Wealth.   I. Reiser, Andrea.   II. Title.
    HF5386.R35 2010
    650.1—dc22

                                                                            2010032271

Printed in the United States of America

10 9 8 7 6 5 4 3 2 1

To Mimi
We miss your sunshine

CONTENTS

10
Courage & Living Without Regrets / 215
Alysa Mendelson Graf: The Courage to Follow Your Heart
Ina Garten: Jumping Off Cliffs

INTRODUCTION

This book was born a very different project. Its genesis was simply an update to a personal finance book we had written as part of a team more than 10 years ago. However, as we began discussing how profoundly the world had changed over the last decade, as well as how our own lives had evolved, we realized the last thing we wanted to spend our time writing was yet another technical tome offering tactical financial advice and outlining investment strategies. If it actually were as easy to make heaps of money as following the advice in personal investing books, given their popularity, wouldn't there be many more millionaires out there? Wouldn't the level of individual debt have dropped significantly?

The more we talked about the book revision, the less noble and useful it sounded to pontificate one-size-fits-most investment advice to hopeful readers. How little—if any—difference would it really make in anyone's life? Moreover, the writing process would distract us from our primary responsibility: making a difference in the lives of our four sons, a lively bunch of teens and tweens who will be out from under our roof in the blink of an eye.

We agreed that if we were going to commit to writing a new book, it should be about something that would be particularly meaningful to our boys, as well as touch others. Inspired by the personal finance area, we initially set out to study the diverse base of several thousand clients that David has cultivated in his 24+ year career as a professional wealth management advisor to see if we could identify common traits or trends among successful investors that would be valuable to pass along.

Interestingly, what we noticed were two distinct investing personalities that we came to refer to as "Fulfilled Investors" and "Discontented Investors." Typical Fulfilled Investors—no matter whether they were wildly wealthy or modestly getting by, whether highly educated executives or hard-working laborers—understood and trusted investment advice; planned judiciously; spent, saved and borrowed prudently; exhibited patience and discipline; set realistic goals and measured success against achieving those goals. On the other hand, Typical Discontented Investors—again, regardless of net worth, education level, or job status—tended to second-guess and mistrust professional financial advice; set unachievable goals; often spent and borrowed irresponsibly to get what they wanted, when they wanted; sought to place blame during tough markets; expected results immediately; became impatient quickly and abandoned plans impulsively.

When we looked deeper, we observed, not coincidentally, that these traits and attitudes spilled into the rest of their lives as well. Clients we had identified as Fulfilled Investors were generally grateful, appreciative, open, trusting, and habitually shared deep satisfaction with their lives, their families, their jobs and activities, essentially making them Fulfilled Individuals. Clients we had identified as Discontented Investors were frequently overbearing, chronically disgruntled, self-pitying, skeptical, entitled, and expressed envy and resentment toward the successes and accomplishments of others. Very little seemed to make these Discontented Individuals happy and they had a habit of jumping constantly from one thing to another in life, seeking unattainable, elusive fulfillment, yet ultimately lacking the patience and gratitude to ever achieve it.

What, then, could we elicit from these empirical observations? When we broke it down, we found that there was a distinct set of virtues and values that Fulfilled Individuals universally seemed to possess, albeit in varying amounts and combinations. They happened to be the same timeless virtues and values that have enabled and empowered Americans on both sides of the aisle to live happy and prosperous lives for more than 200 years—and seemed to be the collective essence for making Fulfilled Individuals, well, fulfilled.

When we looked at people in our own lives—friends, family, and acquaintances—it elucidated even more keenly the role these qualities play in attaining success and happiness. Those we admired all seemed to have their own unique recipe for success, using these qualities as ingredients.

Considering these virtues and values in the larger context of our country and our culture was disheartening; they've all but disappeared from sight these days in the media and in our schools. What were once respected as honorable, aspirational qualities have fallen by the wayside, considered largely unnecessary and unpopular in today's instant gratification culture. It's both sad and shameful to see that so many basic American virtues and values that built this country and fostered individual success have been abandoned. Talent, dignity, and humility are marginalized, while fame—by any means—is the overarching ambition for our youth. An undignified casualness and disrespect is the cultural paradigm in many of our schools. Rampant, baseless litigiousness promotes the concept that you do not need to be accountable for your own actions because there's always someone you can blame for your misfortunes.

With the prevalence of parents who are "too busy" and/or "too tired" to monitor their kids' 24/7 access to mass media and the Internet, traditional role models have essentially been replaced by celebrities and media figures. Rather than learning purposeful lessons from parents, family members, teachers, religious and political leaders, today's impressionable youth instead fill their free time consuming a steady diet of gossipy, morally vacant programming on reality TV and the Internet, featuring both well-known celebrities and unknown wannabes behaving badly. Addiction specialist Dr. Drew Pinsky calls this the "Mirror Effect" in his 2009 book of the same name, defining it as "the process by which provocative, shocking, or otherwise troubling behavior, which has become normalized, expected, and tolerated in our media culture, is increasingly reflected in our own behavior."

Tantalized by every nuance of celebrity, many kids today presume that fame is a birthright, and they bask in the illusion that achieving it brings instant glamour, wealth, attention, power, and adoration. Disturbingly, a 2006 Pew Research Center study showed that 51 percent of 18-to-25-year-old Americans cited fame as the most important or second most important life goal of their generation, exalting celebrity to a defining factor of success in their view. And if they can't be famous themselves, sometimes just being close to a celebrity is enough of an aspiration. Jake Halpern, author of *Fame Junkies: The Hidden Truth Behind America's Favorite Addiction* (Mariner Books, 2006), teamed up with Syracuse University's Newhouse School of Public Communications to poll 650 middle school students in Rochester, New York—a city whose demographics closely reflect those of the United States as a whole—and found that 43.4 percent of the teenage girls surveyed want to become celebrity personal assistants when they grow up. They chose this option twice as often as "the president of a great university like Harvard or Yale," three times as often as "U.S. senator," and four times as often as "the chief of a major company like General Motors."

Yet, so many offensive characters hyped by the media—particularly talentless attention-seeking reality TV stars exploiting their baseless 15 minutes of fame—glaringly seem to lack many of the virtues we ascribe to Fulfilled Individuals. They instead glorify entitlement over personal responsibility. Expending as little effort as possible to squeak by rather than working hard to go above and beyond. Getting rich quick rather than having the patience to build sustainable wealth. Chronically complaining rather than recognizing blessings. Irresponsible indulgence over restraint and sacrifice. Blame instead of accountability. Expectation rather than thankfulness.

Parents perpetually find themselves competing with media and technology for their children's attention, and too often wind up abdicating their responsibility to guide and teach their kids. The more connected and addicted our kids become to media and technology, the less they value face-to-face communication, and it seems that our culture is simply resigned to the inevitability of personal interactions vanishing into extinction. On an April 2010 broadcast of NBC's *Today* show, Ann Curry reported the results of a recent Pew Internet and American Life Project study, showing that a third of U.S. teenagers with cell phones send more than 100 text messages a day, and that texting is now the main way that teens communicate, even more so than phone calls or talking face-to-face. Equally distressing, though, was Curry's offhand concluding comment: "So parents take note, if you want to talk to your kids!"

Sorry, but we're not obliged to accept that as a foregone conclusion. Kids don't have the prerogative to dictate how, when, or what we communicate with them unless we as parents relinquish that privilege. Privately, there's a perceptible buzz to this effect, but publicly, no one is willing to talk about the elephant in the room—or, rather, the country. Parents have seemingly thrown up their hands in frustration and defeat, and often they tiptoe around these issues, becoming reluctant to invoke limits or impose moral guidelines, because they're more worried about their kids' immediate sense of happiness, or because they're desperately afraid to risk losing their children's approval and friendship.

Look, we don't claim to be able to single-handedly change the cultural zeitgeist anytime soon. But we are indeed empowered to change the future moral landscape of our nation—that is, if we collectively dare to step up and parent assertively. We're accountable for raising the next generation of leaders, yet if we stand idly by, lamely bemoan our helplessness, and condone today's pitiful role models exalted by media in pursuit of profits, we'll have no one but ourselves to blame for the further moral decay of our country.

So, what can we do? We can go back to basics. Rediscover the virtues and values that made America a great nation. Reclaim our capacity to parent. Refocus our children's attention. Realign their aspirations toward more noble endeavors. Resolve that taking small steps within our own families can create a powerful change that will make a difference for the future of our kids and our country.

Parenting isn't a hobby; it's a responsibility that requires dedication, commitment, and most notably, communication. You can't "phone it in" as a parent—so "texting it in" is unequivocally out of the question! Without a doubt, parenting is the most important job for our future. The job description covers a wide scope, but a critical portion focuses on building a strong foundation for achieving lifelong happiness and prosperity:

- Set high expectations and model a serious work ethic.
- Value education, honesty, and patience.
- Reward success.
- Encourage informed risk.
- Promote humility and integrity.
- Give kids the tools and emotional support they need, but make them accountable for their accomplishments and actions.
- Teach them how to be resilient and learn from adversity.
- Show them how to be charitably inclined.
- Inspire them not to settle for mediocrity.
- Empower them to have the confidence to challenge substantively but respectfully things they view as incorrect or unjust.
- Help them realize there are short-term repercussions and long-term consequences to choices.
- Expect them to use good manners, and to be kind and thankful.

Of course, there's immeasurably more to parenting than just engaging in this model, but it's a good start to impart these fundamental virtues and values to our kids. Then it's up to them to take those ingredients, mix them up with the freedom and opportunity that this country affords, and write their own recipe for success.

For years, teachers, friends, acquaintances, and even utter strangers have remarked to us that our four boys seem different from other kids in this day and age. "Unique in a really good way," we've heard. What allegedly distinguishes them? Time and again, people cite the fact that they're polite, respectful, and personable. They're responsible, accountable, and independent. They're cheerful, kind, and helpful. They smile, and they look people in the eye when they are speaking to them. We're repeatedly confounded to hear that this is not the norm. All we've tried to do is raise our kids the way each of us was raised; we didn't realize we were nurturing them to be such anomalies. Are they perfect kids? Hardly! Are we perfect parents? Ha!

But people have regularly been so intrigued and curious about what we're doing differently that we've had suggestions that we write a book revealing our secret blueprint for raising or becoming successful, fulfilled individuals. Although we've been humbly flattered, we always chuckled dismissively because we certainly didn't believe we possessed the holy grail. But when we started our research and began to identify the qualities of success found in Fulfilled Individuals, a lightbulb went on. We realized that we are fortunate to surround ourselves and our family with people who are shining examples of these virtues. As it turns out, we've unintentionally been imparting to our kids the importance of these qualities all along—which perhaps in part explains why our boys are continually perceived as being unique.

The sincere truth is, there is no secret to what we're doing. We're merely choosing to exercise our authority as parents rather than letting our kids dictate the rules. We don't live with constant apprehension that our kids won't like us—in fact, they love and respect us more because we strive to help them learn why we believe what we believe. Being consistent with our rules and sharing insight about our decisions gives our boys a strong moral framework that they can carry into everything they do and it helps them put their world in perspective every day.

This book, then, is our solution to the confluence of distressing factors we've outlined. By articulating these virtues and values and explaining how they foster success, we hope to rekindle a national focus on our future by rediscovering invaluable, time-tested tenets from our country's illustrious past. For the essence of sustainable success, wealth, and happiness comes from within.

Introduction

Letters from Home is a wake-up call for all ambitious Americans—regardless of age, social standing, or professional achievement—to reembrace the virtues that build a life of fulfillment and success. Each chapter begins with a letter to our children outlining and describing one or several interrelated virtues and values. We then follow up each letter with profiles introducing you to some exceptional individuals from our lives who personify these qualities. These 20 role models—family members, personal friends, clients, and a few well-known neighbors in our community—are people our boys can actually reach out to, speak with, approach for advice, learn from. As part of our interviews with these successful, fulfilled people, we asked them a series of five questions that we call our "Glimpse Questionnaire" to give you a bit of insight into the person whose profile follows. You will learn from them and about them through their intriguing answers, and their accompanying portraits will further humanize their stories.

Each of these role models supported our premise enthusiastically and unhesitatingly, and we genuinely feel honored to have all of them in our lives. Inspiring as you will likely find these people, they are meaningful and accessible to *our* family. To find your own role models, you merely need to look beyond the TV, the movie screen, the Internet, and into your own life. You will no doubt be humbled by the resplendent resources you are blessed to know personally.

With abounding love for our four sons—and with infinite hope for the success of future generations and our country—we ultimately knew in our hearts that this was the book we were meant to write.

1

EDUCATION

"The more that you read,
the more things you will know.
The more that you learn,
the more places you'll go."

—Dr. Seuss

DEAR BOYS,

In the shrewd words of philosopher John Dewey, "Education is not a preparation for life; education is life itself." One of the greatest gifts you are granted by living in this country is the right to an education, and perhaps the most invaluable and irrevocable gift you can grant yourself is to be a passionate lifelong learner.

Learning is not simply a receptive process of memorizing facts, comprehending lessons, and blindly accepting the information presented to you as absolute truth. Rather, it's an interactive process in which you need to be richly and continually engaged. It is incumbent on you as an invested learner to constantly analyze, question, and discuss information. Search for nuances, new meanings, unique applications. Value formal education, embrace informal opportunities to learn, and take the initiative to go outside the bounds of what's expected and accepted.

We have always viewed ourselves as partners in your education. We were mindful that guiding you to establish sound study practices and take ownership of your work from a young age would be a vital step in becoming independent, active learners in school and throughout life. As parents, our job is to provide you the best learning environment we can and the tools you need to succeed; help you understand the standards and expectations for courses and assignments, as well as the standards and expectations we have established within our own family; and be available to you as resources for explanation, guidance, encouragement, and enrichment. As students, your job is to be habitually inquisitive, intellectually curious, enthusiastic, open-minded, and well-prepared. Becoming a critical thinker—a reflective thinker—a creative thinker—an independent thinker—will serve you grandly not only in your academic studies but in everything you undertake in life.

Ever since you entered preschool as toddlers, we have purposely given you increasing accountability for your education. We have empowered you to advocate for yourselves respectfully in school, and have intentionally tasked you with managing your own schoolwork—because if you routinely depended upon us to help you complete your work, to keep you organized, to set your priorities, and to raise your questions and concerns, you wouldn't be learning and developing fundamental skills that are essential for all of life's endeavors.

Education goes far beyond the four walls of a classroom. Even when formal academic instruction ends, learning never ceases. Having curiosity for the world is what enables you to grow as a human being throughout your lifetime. We have sought to narrate the world for you since you were born, and we strive to expose you to meaningful experiences that we hope will provoke thought, inspire discussion, broaden your knowledge, and cultivate awareness and appreciation.

Even before you started preschool, you had discovered a magical place of learning that introduced you to memorable characters like Corduroy, Madeline, and a family of ducklings that lived in the Boston Public Garden; sent you on exciting adventures to real and imagined worlds like one found at the top of a beanstalk; transported you to the past and the future; and inspired you to make angels in newly fallen snow and bid goodnight to the moon. That place was the public library, an important backbone of our information structure. By providing affordable access to a managed collection of resources and archives, libraries democratize knowledge, and you recognized from an early age that a library card is a passport to limitless information and learning within books, magazines, newspapers, professional and scholarly journals, encyclopedias, computers, CDs, and DVDs. You also appreciate the personal assistance a librarian offers in your quest for knowledge—suggesting interesting reading, guiding you to pertinent research resources, and training you to use technology most advantageously.

Exploring the world is another way to experience learning. By traveling, you continually have the opportunity to learn so much about the world in terms of history, geography, and the diversity of cultures and customs. One of the most powerful trips we've taken as a family was to Washington, D.C., where each of you learned about our country's founding. Getting an up-close view of American history was deeply memorable and informative and sparked spirited family discussions about the Constitution, our government, and the political process. The visit prompted you to research key historical figures and events, helping you to further grasp our country's founding, make emotional connections and observations about our nation, and ask questions about the future. While admittedly you can learn about U.S. history by reading a textbook or listening to a lecture, it doesn't truly come alive until you absorb the breathtaking majesty of the Capitol Rotunda, observe the faded ink that adorns the original Declaration of Independence at the National Archives, or experience the solemn poignancy of the changing of the guard at the Tomb of the Unknowns at Arlington National Cemetery.

You constantly have your eager eyes open for interesting and exciting learning opportunities around you. You have learned about food, math, and science through our family cooking project, in which we'd choose recipes to create together, and then record our observations and reactions on our blog. We used your love for baseball as inspiration to start a family fantasy league, and you learned about statistics, the history and rules of the sport, and what a critical role each player on a team serves. Participating in Little League baseball and other sports has reinforced the significance of teamwork and instilled in you the importance of putting forth your best effort.

Visiting museums and zoos has enlightened you about innumerable fascinating subjects including art, science, history, civilizations, nature, habitats, transportation, fashion, culture, and media. By attending live theatrical performances, you have developed a genuine appreciation for acting, dance, and music, as well as the technical aspects of performance art like direction, sound, lighting, scenic design, costumes and props. Experiencing a variety of musical genres has been illuminating for you, and you were as captivated by the brilliance of master classical violinist Itzhak Perlman at the New York Philharmonic as you were by the exuberant talent of the tribe of hippies howling at the moon in *Hair* on Broadway.

Attending religious school has enabled you to understand your faith and ancestry in the context of history, as well as other religions and spiritual concepts. Your Jewish summer camp experience has not only enriched your religious learning, but has fostered your independence and self-confidence. Performing in ensemble acting groups has taught you about public speaking, which is a critical skill you will continually need to engage and refine throughout your lives.

Although you may not know it, you have even learned during the most mundane activities. Going to Dad's office or Papa's shipyard or the supermarket teaches you about commerce and industry. A fun day at the beach offers you the opportunity to learn about waterways, tides, the sun, sea life, wind, and weather.

Simply looking up at a starlit night sky has spurred you to study and learn about celestial objects in the vast universe. And for our family, rides in the car—whether five minutes to school or hours on a long journey—always provide treasured learning time together. Since the days when you were tiny infants strapped into car seats, we've taken advantage of the captive, uninterrupted environment to do everything from sing Black Eyed Peas songs, to imitate *Family Guy*'s Stewie Griffin, to explain how location affects real estate pricing, to lecture on the consequences of underage drinking.

Technology and media have given you the ability to access information and satisfy your curiosity almost instantaneously. Yet you need to realize that instant access also presents the challenge and responsibility of continually filtering overwhelming amounts of information to distinguish fact from opinion, and evaluating the credibility of sources in terms of bias, accuracy, reputability, and currentness. Use these powerful tools wisely, and rely on the information you gather to enrich independent thought, not replace it.

Knowledge is fluid, and you never know where it can lead. It builds on itself, impelling you to imagine possibilities and solutions with innovation and ingenuity, and it keeps us on an evolutionary path. No one in our life embodies this message more passionately than the acclaimed and esteemed principal of your high school, John Dodig. He speaks out in the following profile about the educational reform necessary to keep our country competitive, and he's a bell ringer for a concerted national effort to emphasize the paramount importance of education for all Americans. We know you appreciate how fortunate you are that Mr. Dodig inspires your academic lives every day.

With love,
Mama and Dad

JOHN DODIG

What's the best advice you've ever gotten?

Don't underestimate what a principal can do.

If you were to receive an award, what would you want it to be for?

Helping to change someone's life.

Who or what inspires you?

The realization that the position I hold is very powerful, in that it can affect in a positive way the individual lives of people in a school.

What do you see as the greatest challenge for the next generation of Americans?

The economic survival of this country.

What three (famous) people, living or dead, would you invite to your fantasy dinner party?

Oprah Winfrey
Bono
Jesus Christ

J ohn Dodig is on a crusade to make education cool.

And, he says, it's got to be a collective initiative between parents, educators, political leaders, sports figures, musicians, actors, and other celebrities, to effectively influence the media message. "The problem is not an educational issue as much as it is a social issue," he asserts, "but few of our national leaders are willing to say that publicly."

Principal of Staples High School in Westport, Connecticut, the top public high school in the state, John proposes, "Imagine if someone in this country was able to motivate the movie, television, music, and advertising industries to make education the aspiration of every young person." He continues, "Imagine what our country would be like if those millions of kids who have always been poorly educated became obsessed with the notion that being educated, going to college, and mastering the skills of life-long learning were the best ways to fame, wealth, and the good life, whereas pursuing a path that leads to being a basketball, football, rap, television, or movie star may not always lead to the happiest or healthiest life."

Without a good education, John doesn't see a particularly bright future for America's middle class. "One hundred years ago, if you lived in a major urban area there was poverty and there were gangs just as there are now," he notes. "Huge numbers of young people dropped out of school or graduated high school with barely a basic knowledge of reading, writing, and mathematics. Unfortunately, some of these young people eventually wound up dead. Some wound up in jail." He goes on, "But many others saw the light at some point in their lives and decided to get a job in a factory. They learned a skill, joined a union, made decent money, raised a family, moved to a place like Levittown, and slowly became middle class. They stayed with the company until retirement and during that time sent their children to college to become professionals."

According to John, however, that strategy just doesn't cut it anymore: "We don't need people trained to bolt four tires onto a car for 35 years. Robots do that. We don't build washing machines. They are built in other countries."

And much as the media might have young people believe otherwise, the solution doesn't lie in pursuing fleeting fame. The answer, John believes, lies in becoming well-educated.

"Every student now needs to be able to think critically, work in small groups to solve problems, use mathematics at a level of at least precalculus, demonstrate an understanding of both the physical and biological sciences, and master the art of learning," insists John, "because it is something they will have to continue to do for the rest of their lives."

John firmly believes that education is the key to success and prosperity, affording flexibility and adaptability—two skills John sees as crucial for the next generation. To validate his impassioned perspective, he frequently references an October, 2009 *New York Times* op-ed column by Thomas Friedman titled "The New Untouchables." In the piece, Friedman insightfully explains that today's students need to learn a new level of thinking out of the box in order to be globally competitive, and that it's up to our nation's public schools to provide the right education to produce these innovators and creative thinkers.

"These kids need the ability to think on their feet, solve problems, and learn something new at the drop of a hat," John contends. "So my corporation goes out of business? I don't care, I'll get another job. Or 'You're not going to make widgets anymore, you're going to make that? Fine. Give me the manual. I'll read it; I'll teach myself how to do it.'"

One of the first steps, in John's opinion, is to adopt corporate hiring practices in the public education field to attract dynamic leaders to be principals at elementary, middle, and high schools, and make the pay competitive with the corporate scale.

"It has to be the right fit for the school, and you need to look for the absolute best people—just like you would in looking for a CEO of a corporation or the president of the United States," he reasons. "And then you have to pay them a lot, because many of the people who have those traits will choose business because they can make $300,000, $400,000, $500,000 a year and all the stipends that go with it . . . you become a principal somewhere, you might make $65,000 a year."

Without strong leadership in the schools, John sees the health of the country at stake. "We believe that dynamic leaders can affect change. We see that all the time in the newspapers—'Principal changes this school' and 'Teacher changes that classroom'—so we know it can happen," he maintains. "Then let's go out and find these people. Let's buy these people, pay them double or triple what they're getting—and then let them go change a school."

John, who has devoted his entire 40+-year career to education, points to one of his own childhood teachers as his inspiration to affect kids' lives. A product of what he calls a dysfunctional household, John didn't meet his father until he was four because of the war, and says he was afraid of the man from the moment he walked in the door. He describes bitter tension in his home life as a child, and remembers his parents being engaged in constant battles. His father's repeated business failures caused the family to uproot numerous times, moving throughout New York and Connecticut, and eventually his parents divorced.

"The only person who had a profound effect on me as a child was Mr. Wilner, my fourth- and fifth-grade teacher at PS 186 in

Queens," recalls John. "He was the male role model in my life since I couldn't stand my father. He made learning exciting for us." He continues, "There was something about the guy that I needed in my life, so he was my mentor and my surrogate father, just for the six hours every day at school. And I think that's why I became a teacher—because I knew that I wanted to do something like what Mr. Wilner did for me."

That's precisely what he has done as a teacher and administrator at schools in inner cities and affluent suburbs alike. He credits his professional mentor, Dr. Raymond Lemley, with inspiring his much-admired style. The mentorship began when Lemley, then the principal at Daniel Hand High School in Madison, Connecticut, hired John as an assistant principal, after observing the special relationship John had cultivated with the low-income minority students he was teaching at a middle school in New Haven.

John talks about Ray Lemley with great respect and fondness. "He used to stand in front of the building every morning and say hello to everybody, and he got to know as many kids as he possibly could. He wasn't afraid to get in their face, and he always had something nice to say to somebody. His belief was, 'Anything is possible, if you believe strongly in it, and you model it.'"

This philosophy made an indelible impression on John, who greets as many of the 1,800 Staples students as possible as they come into school every morning. He believes it's critical for him and his administrative staff to really get to know the students for a number of reasons. First, he wants to model for teachers and students a caring, supportive environment, which makes the school a safe place to learn, think, challenge, and question. "I think a lot of that is going to hit the kids years after they leave us," he suggests. "I don't know if they can articulate it now, but caring for one another and accepting one another is modeled in this school. I think that kids will eventually understand that it was something special that benefited them, and when they get into a professional position some day, then they will hopefully try to recreate that same kind of environment for their team."

John feels it's most meaningful not only to show his love for his teachers and students, but to tell them as well. "I tell my faculty when I meet with them," he shares. "I told the senior class last year, 'I love being here. I love each of you.' They all applauded and that brought tears to my eyes."

John also makes sure that each day he takes the opportunity to say something kind and complimentary to students as he sees them around the school. "I do it intentionally, because I'm the principal and it's a big deal to them," he says. "The principal of the high school can be a position that the kids admire, but not all principals are admired—you have to earn it."

He also goes to great lengths to foster kindness because, as he confides, "If somebody likes you, they are more likely to do what you ask them to do." John strives to hire teachers who want their students to like them, and in turn, he wants his teachers to genuinely like him. "That doesn't mean that I'm going to play golf with them, or poker every Thursday night—I don't socialize with my teachers," he explains. "But of course I want them to like me, because then when I say, 'Can we work on this new goal?' they'll buy into it—and in the end it helps 1,800 kids."

Further, he believes that by deterring student anonymity, administrators can pick up on subtle and not-so-subtle changes in a student who may benefit from intervention by someone at the school. "If the community is willing to provide enough adults in the building so kids are not anonymous—so that you know every kid—someone will know when a kid is behaving or dressing different than she or he was before. But that's a people-intensive enterprise," he acknowledges.

John knows, however, that like his old teacher Mr. Wilner, a teacher or principal's supportive influence often lasts only as long as the student is at school. In areas where education is generally not valued, particularly in inner cities and rural America, John laments that many kids go home to environments where their affective needs are not met. "It's hard when there's nobody there. Or there may be somebody there who wants to be able to help, but just can't. So these kids go back into misery, squalor, drug-addled environments," he presumes. "I guess somebody will rise out of that, but the preponderance of them will be just like their parents."

According to John, if we want to change the life path for these kids, we need to barrage them during their time away from school with the constant, consistent message that education is essential to this country, and to the well-being of every citizen in the United States.

"If every politician, every time they spoke—everywhere—about anything, wove that into what they were saying, things would change," he alleges. "The message has to be every day to those kids—everything they watch on TV, every comment made by basketball players, football players—has to be education. I think it's their responsibility. Every day. Every day. And it would change the lives of those kids," he proclaims.

John cites mass media support for the anti-smoking movement during the 1980s as an example of successful social and cultural change. "How did we get the movie industry to sell tickets and make money when you never saw a star in a movie smoking a cigarette? And in that time, coincidentally, everybody gave up smoking," he reflects. "We did that in 20 or 25 years. Talk about profound social change! It worked. It changed culture in America profoundly. Why can't we do the same thing to send the message that education is important? We are good at sending messages to young people. Why not this one?" he asks.

If the message about the importance of education reached young Americans, John reasons that kids would show up at school eager and determined to learn, and the very schools that are now being maligned would be able to accomplish what they all want to and can provide for their students. "This is something that we can do as a nation," he insists. "Why not give it a varsity try on a national scale?"

2

HARD WORK

"The big secret in life is that there is no big secret. Whatever your goal, you can get there if you're willing to work."

–Oprah Winfrey

GREETINGS GENTS,

Once upon a time, hard work was part of the fabric of our country. Rather than looking for a shortcut to success, people believed that "industry"—hard work, determination, energy, effort, perseverance, patience—was the yellow brick road to achieving the American Dream. So why does it seem like the American Dream has become more of an entitlement than something to work for?

Historically, Americans focused on a combination of thrift and hard work as a means to accumulate money. Early settlers like the New England Puritans, Pennsylvania Quakers, and other Protestant sects were instilled with a Protestant work ethic—the belief that financial success was Divine indication of the holiness of hard work. In colonial times, Benjamin Franklin harped on the value of industry in *Poor Richard's Almanack*, crafting such pithy aphorisms as "If we are industrious, we shall never starve," "Industry pays debts, while despair increaseth them," and "Diligence is the mother of good luck, and God gives all things to industry." Abraham Lincoln championed the American North expressly for defending the principle that industry promoted opportunity for all men to prosper. In the years of hardship that followed the American Civil War, people found comfort and hopefulness in the works of author Horatio Alger, whose rags-to-riches tales portrayed boys overcoming their inauspicious beginnings through hard work and discipline to achieve the American Dream of wealth and success.

The Industrial Age, however, altered the work ethic in the second half of the 19th century, as factories capable of mass production essentially replaced home and workshop trades. The independence, creativity, and personal production that had motivated skilled artisans vanished, disheartening the semiskilled workers who were now responsible for operating single-task machines that performed but a small piece of the manufacturing process. Factory workers were supervised and regulated, consequently losing their sense of control over their own destinies, and the repetitive nature of machine work led to a lack of intellectual stimulation in the labor force.

As the Information Age dawned in America in the early 1980s, the manufacturing jobs that had reliably employed American workers for over a century began to move overseas to significantly less costly workforces, shifting the country into a service economy. The new technology-influenced jobs were more complex than manufacturing jobs, and required engaged thinking and decision making. Workers needed higher levels of education to perform these jobs, as well as develop skills like the ability to solve problems, manage teams, and continually source and apply cutting-edge information to projects and tasks. Information Age jobs gave workers control over their productivity, greater self-expression, and a more fulfilling sense of empowerment, making a work ethic more relevant than in the Industrial Age. Ambitious, educated college graduates entered the workforce with high aspirations, expecting to work hard and advance rapidly, but there was sometimes a dispiriting impatience if upward progress didn't happen as quickly as they had anticipated.

This sense of disappointment in delayed gratification became more widespread throughout the 1990s, as technology advanced and became affordable to the masses. Conveniences like fax machines, mobile phones, overnight delivery services, and Internet access conditioned people to expect immediate connection and information, and enhancements like smartphones and on-demand television have only exacerbated the presumption that we're entitled to everything instantly—resulting in a culture that has grown impatient at having to wait for anything. Since all four of you were born in the 1990s, you have no frame of reference for life before these developments, just an expectation and trust that technology will continue to evolve, further simplifying tasks and accelerating productivity.

Concurrent with the advancement of technology came a rise in the popularity of cable television, along with an explosion of new television networks with hours of programming to fill. In 1985, there were 31 million cable television subscribers in the United States, and now 25 years later, that figure has more than tripled, with over 100 million households subscribing to some form of pay TV. To maximize profits and minimize the need for costly professional actors and writers, programmers turned to formats like documentary-style shows following police on patrol, personal stories featuring couples getting married or giving birth, home renovation and interior design shows, talk shows, game shows, cooking shows, talent competition shows, dating shows, and fashion makeover shows—none of which needed professionals to fill the roles of "stars." As Jake Halpern theorizes in his 2006 book, *Fame Junkies: The Hidden Truths Behind America's Favorite Addiction*, "All of this creates a perception, and to some extent a reality, that it is now much easier to become famous. This perception is only bolstered by the emergence of reality TV, which ostensibly makes people famous for simply 'being themselves.'"

Add to that a constant media saturation of celebrity-focused TV shows and publications, and outlets like YouTube, Facebook, Twitter, and other online outlets from which to try to launch a career, and you can see why there's a prevalent perception that fame and celebrity is indeed attainable. Especially appealing is becoming an overnight sensation with little suffering or sacrifice—for everything from demonstrating genuine talent on a competitive TV show, to shooting off your mouth on a reality show, to doing something absurd or vulgar in a viral video. A 2005 nationwide survey conducted jointly by the *Washington Post*, the Henry J. Kaiser Family Foundation, and Harvard University found that two-thirds of high-school-age teens say there's a good chance they will be rich someday, and nearly one-third also predicted they will be famous. Concludes Halpern, "Because fame seems so accessible, delusions of fame don't seem delusional. And when you grow up and join the workplace, you don't want to do drudge work, and you feel disillusioned when that doesn't happen."

The expectation of fast-tracking the road to fame has substantially eroded the traditional concept of the need for hard work and industry, and has made the American Dream seem almost an entitlement rather than something to have to persevere toward. President Barack Obama addressed this issue head-on when he spoke to our nation's schoolchildren in September of 2009, remarking, "I know that sometimes you get the sense from TV that you can be rich and successful without any hard work—that your ticket to success is through rapping or basketball or being a reality TV star, when chances are, you're not going to be any of those things. But the truth is, being successful is hard."

There's simply no way around it. Hard work is just that: hard! It's a learned habit that requires discipline and patience. Showing up, not just phoning it in. Being willing to do whatever needs to be done, whether you love every minute of it or not. No job is beneath someone who is motivated to succeed. The dream, of course, is to do what you are passionate about and the money will follow. The reality is that you have to do what you are passionate about exceedingly well and work tirelessly and wisely in order to create success. Most successful people didn't get where they are by adopting an attitude of trying to get away with doing as little as possible, hoping for a stroke of luck, or wishing for someone to wave a magic wand.

No matter what you choose to do later in life, developing a strong work ethic will help you in any profession. As students, you have already discovered the merits and rewards of hard work. You all continually set high standards for yourselves in your schoolwork, giving it your best shot whether you like the assignment or not, and you've seen your above-and-beyond effort reflected in good grades, academic recognition awards, and acceptance into competitive academic programs. For the last two years, three of you have worked diligently at part-time jobs at your religious school. You spend hours at the piano, practicing until you are satisfied that you have created beautiful music. You've taken swing after swing in the batting cages, adjusting your stance, your grip, and your follow-through until you find the sweet spot. You stay up late into the night tweaking and polishing your articles for the school newspaper so you can submit them by deadline time. For full disclosure, your discipline with household chores occasionally leaves something to be desired (ahem), but when you invest yourselves wholeheartedly in a task, you inevitably achieve excellent results and personal fulfillment.

Dad has valued hard work since he was a little boy, and caught on very early that need creates motivation and incentive.

His parents worked hard in their restaurant business, yet struggled financially, and Dad learned that it was up to him to earn his own spending money. When he was 7, his family moved to a house across the street from a strawberry field, where he got his first job picking berries for five cents a quart. It took until the next summer for Dad to muster the stamina to work from dawn 'til dusk to pick 100 quarts in a day, and he still says it was the best $5 he ever earned. At age 10, he convinced his dad to let him cultivate a quarter-acre garden in the backyard, where he planted and sold fruit and vegetables. He worked the land so diligently as an eager young boy that he eventually earned enough money to split with his dad the cost of a riding lawn-mower—which helped him launch a lawncare business at age 14. He proudly remembers using some of his profits to buy a record player and speakers. When he was 15, Dad got a job during the school year as a dishwasher and busboy at a local restaurant, and he saved his earnings for college. He doesn't remember a time in his life when he wasn't using his industriousness, resourcefulness, and perseverance to earn money.

The person we have chosen to profile on the topic of hard work made an especially profound impression on you boys. Each time you've walked to the nearby Amagansett Farmers Market to pick up some fresh produce or delicious baked treats, you've been repeatedly astounded to find the owner, Eli Zabar—an esteemed icon of the New York City gourmet food world—wearing his white apron and scrambling busily around the store. You've seen him moving crates of vegetables and fixing the refrigeration case, and you were honored and delighted one day to carry home a pound of smoked salmon hand-sliced by Mr. Zabar himself! But as we've gotten to know him, we've discovered that it was not unusual at all to find Mr. Zabar working tirelessly at one of his shops, doing whatever task needed to be done, for it's through his keen industry that he built his tiny fledgling food shop into a celebrated epicurean empire. You'll be amazed at what two hands and an inspired attitude can accomplish.

Keep your noses to the grindstone,
Mama and Dad

ELI ZABAR

What's the best advice you've ever gotten?

Keep your own counsel.

If you were to receive an award, what would you want it to be for?

Maintaining integrity while achieving my goals.

Who or what inspires you?

Working with my hands and seeing possibilities.

What do you see as the greatest challenge for the next generation of Americans?

Conveying moral and social values to the next generation given the societal breakdown of the family.

What three (famous) people, living or dead, would you invite to your fantasy dinner party?

My father
My grandfather
My future grandson or great-grandson

HARD WORK REAPS REWARDS

How can one lone man manage to grow a small, specialty food shop into a gourmet food empire? If you're a tireless, creative visionary like Eli Zabar, you can accomplish anything you want with hard work.

Now in his late 60s, Eli is the youngest of the three Zabar brothers born to Russian immigrants Louis and Lillian Zabar. Eli was just 7 years old when his father died in 1950. His considerably older brothers, Saul and Stanley, took over the operation of the appetizing store their father had opened on Broadway at 80th Street in New York City, selling the highest quality smoked fish and house-roasted coffee, while young Eli went to school and helped out in the store at night.

"Both my brothers have always been really, really hardworking people. And in completely different ways," he observes. "So I probably felt I had to run as fast as I could to catch up. I had an awful lot of admiration for my brothers," he continues. "They're much older than me—12, 14 years older. I wanted to be like them, and at the same time I really wanted to be my own person."

Although all three brothers attended private school, Eli was nearly a generation removed from the world his brothers grew up in. As such, he was shaped by a more upper-middle class upbringing as part of a generation that had more creative professional aspirations.

"By the time I got to private school, kids weren't becoming doctors and lawyers, they were becoming research scientists and poets and playwrights," he says.

As a student at Columbia University, Eli worked at Zabar's as the night shift manager. His brothers, meanwhile, brought in an outside partner to help run the retail store. A quintessential youngest brother, Eli was always raring to go, eager to take the business in new directions; however, his more conservative brothers preferred moving forward with baby steps. Consequently, when Eli graduated, he says there wasn't room for him in the operation.

"It was too small a business to accommodate another family member. And since they were much, much older than I was, they certainly weren't going to give me any sort of real respect," he maintains. "Plus, I liked working on my own."

So Eli left the family business and took a job at a grocery wholesaler. There, he began to make sales contacts, eventually developing an extensive network of food industry professionals including chefs, restaurant owners, and other sources. Within several years, he decided it was time to set up his own shop, and in July of 1973 he launched his flagship restaurant, a gourmet deli and café called E.A.T. on Madison Avenue. The venerable eatery still showcases his original ideas today.

Eli was deeply motivated by travel through Europe in the early 1970s. His inspiration for E.A.T. was a food shop in London. "I admired everything about that shop. They had these pretty girls cooking in this little shop, and they all wore little aprons and spoke with English accents, and the food they made was pristine and quite delicious." He goes on, "The owner would go to the market in the morning and go shopping, and I thought, 'That's who I want to be.'"

E.A.T. opened with just Eli and a dishwasher. Eli fondly recalls, "I loved it. I loved coming in every morning at six o'clock and setting up the store and getting everything ready before the customers came in at eight. I worked the whole day by myself. And that was my favorite part of being in business."

As time went on, however, the operation became too onerous for one person to handle, no matter how hard he worked, and Eli hired a few employees. "That gave me time to experiment and really learn how to do things," he reflects with a smile, his bright blue eyes dancing. "I'd get excited. I'd read books. I would go traveling and go see things."

Again, he brought back unique ideas and new standards from his travels. "I realized there was a whole world out there and nobody really knew about it. I learned how food should taste and what it should look like, and I would come back and try to create or recreate what was in my mind."

As he explored the world and found top-quality edibles, he continually raised his standards for the products he wanted to offer in his shop. Often, suppliers balked at his exceptionally high quality expectations. "I didn't like what was coming in. The product wasn't good enough, and I would send it back," he recalls. "And the common refrain I'd hear was, 'Well it's fine for everybody else, why isn't it fine for you?' There was some-what of a battle going on between what I wanted to do—the way I thought things should be done—and what everybody else accepted."

Instead of settling for mediocrity, the ever-industrious Eli thought out of the box and set out to find his own resources that would meet his standards. "I would say, 'Why argue any further with them? I'll import my own cheeses—the cheese that I want to import,'" he recounts.

No matter what obstacle he encountered, Eli persisted and found a way to accomplish whatever he envisioned and expected. If the cheeses arriving by boat weren't fresh enough, he would arrange for them to be sent by air. When he was told that importers would never sell to such a small company, he set out to find an agent himself. "I said, 'I'll find somebody who is hungry. Somebody who wanted to do business with somebody in New York, who would pay the guy's bills,'" he explains.

When he found himself disheartened with the quality of bread available in New York, Eli experimented endlessly with ingredients and techniques to develop a recipe that measured up to his standards, eventually creating his stone-ground whole wheat Health Loaf. Still underwhelmed, he continually consulted with experts to improve the breads he was making at E.A.T. and selling to local restaurants. In 1992 he opened Eli's Bread, a 15,000-square-foot bakery, where today 105,000 pounds of flour a week is used for bread that is sold to almost 1,000 restaurants, hotels, and markets.

Eli envisioned a unique market where the majority of the products were made on the premises, and he realized that vision in 1993 when he opened Eli's Vinegar Factory, a grocery store and café on 91st Street, in what was New York's last facility for producing mustards and vinegar. Two years later, in a quest to grow fresh salad greens and tomatoes locally, Eli installed greenhouses on the roof of the Vinegar Factory. It is now known as one of the most productive year-round urban agriculture projects, growing a variety of fruits, vegetables, and herbs sold in Eli's stores and used in creating house-made prepared foods.

In 1998, Eli added Eli's Manhattan, a 20,000-square-foot European-style market, to his growing epicurean empire. Inspired by the food halls of Europe, the enormous, two-level shop features a fish market, a butcher department with a windowed aging room, local and organic produce, a global array of cheeses, house-made breads and pastries with a separate kosher bakery, caviar, house-roasted coffee, house-made prepared foods, a flower shop, an adjacent restaurant/café, and a wine shop.

Today Eli Zabar is a veritable New York institution, and he employs around 700 people among his various operations. Yet to this day, he still itches to work with his hands. That was one of the formative reasons he entered into a creative partnership with the Peconic Land Trust to reopen the shuttered Amagansett

Farmers Market on Long Island's East End in 2008. "It was a chance for me to go back and actually work like I used to work when I first started," he confesses.

He also saw the Amagansett project as an opportunity to spend time with his college-age twin sons. "I thought it would be a project that the kids and I could do together, whether it was the whole summer or part of the summer," he shares. "The kids were really vital in helping open it, and it was a great experience."

Eli has purposely taught his boys by example the value of hard work since they were quite young. "The boys have always worked the big holidays—Jewish holidays and Christmas and New Years and Thanksgiving—from the time they were maybe seven. They didn't get paid for it, the idea was that was the payback for our lifestyle," he says. "Now they do get paid because they know something and they're contributing, so they work here during the holidays."

Eli's wife, Devon Fredericks, also works with him, running the gift basket division, so naturally much of the talk at home centers on the business. "Since they were born, the boys have absorbed a lot just by listening. It's part of the matrix of the family," he notes. "We're very open. How much money we make. Where the expenses are. How we go about giving bonuses. Where we have formulas. Where we don't. They've learned that our wealth is based on our business, and that it didn't happen magically. We earned it."

He and his wife have both always wished for their sons to enjoy working as much as they do. "We've said it out loud to them and quietly to ourselves that when they go to work, we hope they go because they really want to be here. That they really love what they're doing. That they're challenged by it. That they look forward to it," he shares.

Perpetually motivated by possibilities, Eli thrives on generating new ideas and better ways to do things. "Every day I feel there are so many things that are left undone, and that I'm still trying to get right. We change a display, we make a new recipe—whatever it is we're working on—and that makes everything else in place have to change, too," he acknowledges. "So I'm constantly feeling like things are never done completely or properly. And so tomorrow is another day. We get another shot. We get another bite of the apple."

He admits he's happiest when he realizes that there's a possibility he didn't see. "I'll be satisfied for a while, but then I'll suddenly get a spark of an idea that could be done and all the combinations and permutations that go along with it, and then I'm extremely happy," reports Eli. "I used to say to my wife in the morning, 'You know, I have an idea,' and she used to say, 'Oh, not again!'"

Since childhood, this hardworking entrepreneur has strived to be active and work with his hands. "I never really liked school because I found it almost impossible to sit in classes during the day," he remembers. "I couldn't wait 'til the gym period came. What today is called attention-deficit disorder, my mother's word for it was the Yiddish 'shpilkes.'"

According to Eli, operating his own business for all these years has provided an excellent outlet for his shpilkes. "It's allowed me to be continually busy, to explore things. And there's never a moment to be bored. There's always something that has to be done."

Despite his position at the helm of this extraordinarily successful enterprise, no job is too menial for Eli, from mopping the floor to fixing a refrigeration case. He emphasizes, "I don't put a value on whether one job is more important or more valuable, and another job is less valuable." The boss also doesn't distinguish between weekends and weekdays. "Being in the retail business, there's no difference between Saturday/Sunday and Monday/Tuesday. We never took the weekends off, even from the time I opened for business," he confirms. "And we've never taken Christmas off because it's a retail business."

Carrying on the family tradition, Eli Zabar has turned his name into a highly acclaimed iconic brand. With indefatigable resourcefulness, boundless ideas—and his own two hands—he has more than accomplished his mission to be like his brothers, yet really be his own person.

— *3* —

RECOGNIZING OPPORTUNITY

"Sometimes you just gotta say, 'What the heck.'"
—Joel Goodsen's father, in *Risky Business*

Hɪ Guʏs,

Wouldn't it be swell if a FedEx truck pulled up to the house every so often and delivered a package addressed to you that was bedecked in dazzling flashing lights, and when you opened it, an exciting siren sounded and amid heaps of colorful confetti was a specially marked box of opportunity? Sigh. If only opportunity was so glaringly obvious to identify and capture.

Life presents infinite opportunities. Every day you get the chance to build, create, connect, love, appreciate, thank, forgive, help, grow, teach, apologize, explore. It's a matter of how alert you are to opportunity and how prepared you are to act on it that makes the difference. Often it appears out of the blue—and just as often it disappears as swiftly as it arrived, because someone more agile was able to swoop in and seize it, or conditions changed and it's no longer feasible.

Seemingly lucky people are not really luckier than anyone else, they are simply more ready to grab chances that come their way. Says Oprah Winfrey, "I believe luck is preparation meeting opportunity. If you hadn't been prepared when the opportunity came along, you wouldn't have been 'lucky.'"

Being prepared to recognize advantageous chances requires being aware and being present—fully engaged in the moment—all the time. Learn everything you can, from anyone you can, any time you can. Make the most of every experience, noting the nuances and temporarily filing them away if they don't seem relevant at the time. Know your skills and strengths, and have the discipline to practice and improve so you are constantly at the top of your game. Believing in yourself and your abilities will help give you the confidence you need to take the leap when opportunity arises.

People frequently miss opportunities because they are too focused on looking for something else—for instance, you might go to a party intent on finding a love interest and miss out on meeting someone who could've been a new friend or an important business connection. The more you open your mind to seeing different possibilities, the more opportunities you will see. In simple terms, consider the duck-rabbit illusion, the famous ambiguous image that can alternately be perceived as a duck's head facing left or a rabbit's head facing right. Suppose on first glance you saw a duck, had no reason to assume there were other possibilities, and stashed the picture away. The next day, someone called you in desperate need of a picture of a rabbit, and was willing to pay $100 for one. As far as you know, you only have a picture of a duck, so you tell the person you can't be of help, and wind up losing out on the $100. If you spend your life never looking beyond the ducks, you're sure to miss out on a lot of rabbits.

It's also imperative to stay aware of the markets, trends, and factors that have even a marginal chance of affecting you. Knowing what's going on in the world, or your industry or your community will help you see possibilities for opportunity. As you may remember, we actively kept a pulse on the local real estate market in 2008 as we bought a new house across town, and expected that our charming, older colonial on premier land in a prestigious neighborhood would sell in a flash. Then the credit crisis hit, and the market for homes in our area, as well as in most of the country, was devastated. We lowered the price of the house to 10 percent below what we had paid only a couple of years earlier, yet the house languished on the market for months without a serious offer. After nearly a year went by, we began to see other potential opportunities for the equity that we had tied up in the old house—namely a flood of vacation homes in resort communities that families needed to sell much below market value, given the difficult recession of 2009. We realized that if we dropped the price of our old colonial enough to stimulate an offer, we could likely pick up a beach property at a bargain price just before the summer began. We instructed our real estate agent to lower the advertised price another 10 percent and, lo and behold, within one week we had a cash offer close to the asking price from a buyer who wanted to close within 10 days. In the meantime, we had been intensely researching real estate in the beach community, so when the deal officially closed, we were able to scoop up a newly built home right by the beach, for about one-third less than the original asking price. Within weeks the real estate market began to see signs of life, and by the end of the summer, the house next door, a nearly identical property being constructed by the same builder, sold for almost 30 percent more than we had paid. By being aware of the real estate market, we were able to make a plan to take advantage of tremendous opportunity that ordinarily we could only dream of.

You are perpetually empowered to create opportunity where one doesn't apparently exist. Use your imagination to think outside the box and develop a unique idea that fills an underserved niche, bucks conventional wisdom, capitalizes on an emerging trend, or revolutionizes a time-tested product or service. Brilliant ideas are constantly born by finding solutions to problems. As Sara Blakely's tale goes, she was a young office equipment sales manager who performed standup comedy at night, and one night in 1998, she was getting dressed for a gig and couldn't figure out what to wear under her white pants that wouldn't show lines. She inventively cut the feet off her panty hose, and found that the resulting footless hosiery did the trick quite nicely. Hearing that many of her friends had done the same thing at one time or another gave Blakely an epiphany. She researched and wrote her own patent for body-slimming, footless pantyhose; came up with the edgy name Spanx, and because she believed in her product and her sales ability, she managed to get such major department stores as Neiman Marcus and Saks Fifth Avenue to carry her product. Soon after, she was overjoyed to learn that Oprah had chosen Spanx as one of her favorite products in 2000, and the endorsement instantly gave the pantyhose priceless exposure to a national audience. By pursuing a solution to a silly, seemingly frivolous problem, Blakely managed to find a niche that launched a company that has grown to retail sales of more than $350 million in less than 10 years.

Often, there's abundant opportunity in adversity. You've heard the expression, "When life hands you lemons, make lemonade." But lemonade clearly isn't the only option—be imaginative, thoughtful, and incomparable in how you put your lemons to use. Don't dwell on what went wrong; instead focus on what you can do to move forward. Otherwise, you may stare so long at the closing door that you may not realize another is opening. Scope out useful information by reading and by listening, and develop relationships with creative people who can be your extended eyes and ears. Put yourself out there and be willing to help others succeed. Rather than telling people what you want to do, show them.

It's critical to have the tools to evaluate opportunity in an objective, judicious, and timely manner and be flexible enough to make sound decisions before the door closes. Explore opportunity from all angles and with an open mind. Entertain unorthodox ideas and hold back natural skepticism. When an opportunity that's outside the norm or beyond your comfort zone presents itself, ignore the instinct to seek out reasons not to pursue it. Focus on your potential instead of your limitations.

One of the most common impediments to recognizing and acting on opportunity is complacency. If you live your life on cruise control, afraid to deviate from your routine, your mind isn't open to opportunities and you'll never be actively alert to them. It takes initiative and courage to break out of the comfort zone that typically insulates us from recognizing opportunity when it arises. But new or random experiences continually introduce the potential for fresh opportunities, and having a positive attitude toward change opens up the world. Sometimes it's necessary to endure temporary sacrifice or discomfort in order to take advantage of an opportunity with a longer-term payoff. You need to look past the short term and keep yourself motivated by focusing on what you eventually stand to gain. As Winston Churchill said, "A pessimist sees the difficulty in every opportunity; an optimist sees the opportunity in every difficulty."

Frankly, you four boys are on this earth precisely because we both always viewed blind dates as opportunities. Mom's attitude was that while she might not ultimately be interested in the guy she was being fixed up with, perhaps she had a friend he'd be perfect for. Or maybe the guy had a cousin who worked in her field and she could make a new business contact. In any case, she always figured it was worth an hour or two of her time to find out. One evening Dad went to an event where he was introduced to a young man named Ed, who had recently gone on a blind date with Mom. Mom hadn't found Ed interesting, but Ed had felt differently and spent the evening telling Dad all about Mom. Intrigued and ever resourceful, Dad found a mutual friend who shared Mom's phone number, and when he mustered the courage to call her out of the blue soon after, the two of us ended up chatting for an hour and a half. When we met in person for our first date a few weeks later, we both knew instantly that we had gone on our last blind dates. We became engaged seven weeks later, and the rest is history!

Someone else you know and love, your Papa, had his eyes open to recognize a business opportunity more than 35 years ago. The story of the evolution of his company is the opening profile for this chapter. The other profile features our friend, Tim Brabham, who married one of Mom's dear pals from high school. Tim is a premiere example of someone who keeps his eyes and ears open for career advancement opportunities, and he and his family are able to act quickly when they encounter promising opportunities because they are open to change and have a positive attitude about new experiences. Recognizing and seizing opportunity has changed the lives of both men and their families for the better.

Carpe diem,

Mama and Dad

DAVID COHEN

What's the best advice you've ever gotten?

Hands-down, it was advice from my mother that even though I had cold feet as a 23-year-old guy—wet behind the ears—I should go through with the wedding and marry my bride.

If you were to receive an award, what would you want it to be for?

Fulfilling my charitable responsibility to the community by giving wealth and service.

Who or what inspires you?

My spouse, my children, and my grandchildren.

What do you see as the greatest challenge for the next generation of Americans?

Honesty of politicians and the advance of socialism, because, as Margaret Thatcher used to say, eventually you run out of other people's money.

What three (famous) people, living or dead, would you invite to your fantasy dinner party?

George Washington
Winston Churchill
David Ben-Gurion

I t was a good thing David Cohen was listening when opportunity knocked in 1974, because when he opened the door, he found a successful business waiting to be built on the other side of the threshold.

A married 35-year-old with three young children at the time, David had been working for a scrap metal company in Providence, Rhode Island, and managing several parcels of industrial property owned by his father and uncles, including a deepwater pier facility. One day out of the blue, David got a call from a local ship's agent asking if he could rent the dock for a merchant ship that needed pipe repair.

"They were going to bring somebody down from Maine to weld up the pipes on the ship," recalls David. "And I said to the agent, 'Gee, I know local welders. You don't need to bring someone way down from Maine. So I called the local welding shop that I knew, and told them to go over to the ship, weld up the pipe, and send me the bill."

The agent also mentioned an energetic young diver he knew named Paul Baker who had been doing ship repair work in Maine and New York, and was now looking for work in the southeastern New England area. As David remembers, "The agent said, 'Maybe you can hire him and he can fix ships.'" At the time, he made a mental note, but didn't stop to think seriously about the possibility.

Just days later, however, he got a call from a second ship's agent about a tanker at the Hess Petroleum terminal in Groton, Connecticut, that needed repair. He instantly thought of contacting the diver whose name had been passed along to him, and as it turned out, Paul Baker was ready and willing to head to Groton, even offering to bring a diving buddy to help out. David, a lifelong boater, put his own 24-foot power boat on a trailer and met the two divers in Groton. "We put the boat in at night," he shares. "They had their diving gear, worked on the repairs, slept on the boat under the arc lights at the terminal, alongside the tanker."

David had to bolt early the next morning to get back to his job at the scrap metal company, entrusting his boat and motor to Paul and his friend. "And as I'm riding home on the train," he remembers, "I'm saying, hmmmm. I think somebody's trying to tell me something. I think there's a business here, fixing ships. And I went back to Providence and I decided that I was going to start a business—plain and stupid as that!" He continues, "We had this pier and I just took a risk. I think I was maybe making $20,000 a year at the scrap company, had healthcare and that was it. But I knew I didn't want to work for somebody else."

Within a month, David quit his job at the scrap company, hired Paul Baker as general manager, and launched his business, which he called Promet Marine Services. "It was just me and Paul and one truck," he chuckles. "And we used to go and what we call, 'hit the ships.'" As he describes it, they would meet merchant ships as they tied up at area docks, and after customs and immigration officials boarded the vessels, David and Paul would go up the gangway searching out the ship's chief engineer. They'd inquire about whether the vessel needed any voyage repairs and they quickly found that there was always work to be done—maybe a pipe in the engine room had rotted or an electric motor needed an overhaul. So they'd find out how long the ship was going to be in port, and would hustle to complete the voyage repairs within that time.

David says he was quite fortunate to be establishing his business just as tankers were being "laid up" because of rising oil prices. Ship agents called looking for long-term dockage for these enormous vessels, and David jumped at the opportunity. "I tied up three 750-foot Arco tankers—100-foot wide—that were out of service for almost a year at $500 a day apiece," he explains. "So that was a good way to get started in business."

As the business grew and David began hiring semiskilled employees to handle repairs on the ships and in the machine shop, he found another area of opportunity—working on Navy vessels in Newport. Promet received Navy clearance and started doing contract work around the same time David brought his brother, Joel, on board as a co-owner to help run the burgeoning business.

"I brought Joel in once we were able to take two modest salaries out of the business, so that I could watch my children grow up and go to graduation parties and attend the community activities," recounts David. "It's a 24/7 business, not a 9-to-5 job. Ships have to get repaired in the middle of the night. It's a service business," he adds.

Bringing his brother in gave David a bit of flexibility, since he has always staunchly believed that an owner has a responsibility to oversee the operation at all times. It's a philosophy he carries to this day. "Someone from ownership, somebody from management always has to be there—my brother or myself. Otherwise, people can go off half-cocked and it's not their money," he notes.

The business continued to evolve as David discovered another unique and profitable opportunity for Promet in the late 1970s: unloading and storing highway deicing salt. The company initially unloaded the ships with shore gear, and then when conveyor ships came along, Promet built hoppers and hired trucks as the ships were discharging. "For at least 15 years, we handled 200,000 or 300,000 tons of highway deicing salt on a toll arrangement for both Morton Salt and Diamond," says David.

Performing emergency service has typically been a highly profitable area for Promet. "You make your money on the emergency jobs," David shares. "The regular day-to-day jobs are like hitting a single. So you keep hitting singles all day long. And eventually there's an emergency job that comes in and you hit a home run and make a few extra bucks."

In 1990 as Desert Storm got underway, Promet received the lucrative opportunity to activate three ready-reserve ships that had been in lay berth in Rhode Island ports. But promptly thereafter, the usual sources of business the company had relied on for the previous 15 years abruptly dried up. "The business changed," concedes David. Voyage repair needs declined, the Navy left Newport, and the salt business migrated down the port to the municipal pier, as the City of Providence undercut dockage rates and wharfage charges to the highway deicing salt suppliers to attract business.

The sharp downturn spelled bankruptcy for a number of shipyards in the northeast, many of which carried heavy debt and had come to depend on Navy contracts for business. It was clearly time for shipyard owners to rethink the direction of the marine repair industry. One Boston shipyard, which did an emergency job on the *Queen Elizabeth 2* in 1992 when it ran aground off Martha's Vineyard, made the losing bet that the future was in large ship business. David and Joel went in the other direction, and instead invested in adapting their yard to accommodate a multiplicity of small vessels. They saw the writing on the wall that merchant ships had become antiquated and were being replaced by tug-barge units, while tankers that had transported petroleum products from the Gulf up to the northeast were history.

"There were fishing boats, tugboats," maintains David. "We decided that there were more tugboats, ferry boats, fishing boats out there than ocean-going craft." Remembering their dad's advice—"when business is lousy, that's when machinery manufacturers want to make sales"—David and Joel acquired a piece of equipment in 1994 that transformed the business.

"We had sat on the money we made in 1990, and we bought this big 300-ton travel lift so we could go after these smaller boats," he recounts. The new boat hoist was the biggest marine hauler made at the time. Affectionately called "Big Red" because of its appearance, the lift got Promet into the business of hauling, repairing, and maintaining tugs, ferries, and fishing boats. With fewer competitors left to handle small vessel needs, business turned around. David's son, Michael, joined the business and starting calling on commercial vessel owners in ports around the northeast, keeping Big Red—and Promet—quite busy.

But as the ever-prudent David says, "In business markets, the peaks are short and steep, and the valleys are long and low." With this prescient philosophy, the brothers have long been disciplined to conserve money during busy times in anticipation of slower business cycles. "We don't spend all our dollars," emphasizes David. "We conserve our dollars. We shelter our dollars by depreciation. All you're doing is delaying taxes, but it forces you to buy new machinery and equipment, which then keeps you in business."

Saving for a rainy day paid off again in 2002. "We have always bought machinery when the markets are down low," explains David. He had traveled to Singapore a year or two before to look at a larger boat lift, and had made a couple of unsuccessful bids on the equipment. The manufacturer of the lift, Marine Travelift, was aware of David's interest in a bigger boat hoist, and because the economy was suffering and their own business was down, they came to him with a deal. "They were going to build a 400-metric-ton machine for Delta Yachts out on the West Coast. And they said, 'We'll build a second machine for you, and make you a hell of a deal,'" he recalls. "And on top of it they took our 300-ton machine in trade."

Promet had already fully depreciated Big Red, but the machine was still worth $500,000 in trade. With a 35 percent investment tax credit available on the purchase of the new lift at that time, plus an additional 20 percent depreciation for the first year of five-year straight-line depreciation, the new machine, which cost just under $1.5 million, hit Promet's books for roughly $450,000. As David says, "There's always opportunity when things are bad."

Because the new machine would take 9 or 10 months to build, and Promet wanted to take advantage of the soon-to-expire tax incentive, David made sure the machine would be delivered by August of 2003. "What happens with most people is they wait until the markets are great and then they order the new machine," David observes. "In the commodity business, by the time you order the machine it takes 9, 10 months to build that machine. They generally have to go on foundations and foot-ings and things like that, which you install when the machines are being made," he explains. "By the time the machine comes in, gets erected, and gets put into use, it's already 12, 14 months later. In the commodity business, the markets have changed."

David was schooled to take the reverse approach and buy at the bottom of the market. "When the markets are in the toilet, that's when you order new machinery. And by the time it's deliv-ered, erected, tested, and ready to use, it's already a year or so later and hopefully business has turned around."

David also looks to score bargains at equipment auctions when the economy is troubled. "Again, back in 2002, 2003, there was a lot of great machinery going to the auctions," he recalls. "And we would buy forklifts, scissor lifts, diesel welders for 20 or 30 cents on the dollar. You'd buy $10,000 welders for $5,000. You'd buy $30,000 aerial lifts for $10,000."

By keeping a constant finger on the pulse of the ever-changing business environment and being willing to adapt and take advan-tage of market conditions, David built that flicker of an idea back in 1974 into a company long recognized as a leader in the ship repair industry. Promet now employs 50 people steadily, and up to 100 in peak times. The fortuitous introduction to the young diver who worked on the tanker in Groton more than 35 years ago was a gift, as Paul Baker is still Promet's general manager. Plans for the next evolution of the company include building a 1,200- to 1,500-metric ton floating dry dock at the facility to accommodate ocean-going tugs and other vessels that are heavier than the 400-ton marine lift can handle.

Now semiretired, David is thankful to have had the opportunity to establish and run a successful family-owned business. "The fact that we have this deepwater pier facility allowed us to go into a unique business that not everybody can go into," he shares. "It limits the competition because not everybody has these types of facilities that are needed for this particular type of business—it's not as though you can just start this particular business on any street corner."

He and his brother trade off frequent vacation time these days, and the partnership has allowed each to be able to travel and appreciate leisure activities, knowing the other is holding down the fort. "We've made a modest living all these many years, educated our children, paid the tuition bills, taken vacations, and enjoyed life," David says, appreciating the fulfilling balance between work and life the business has afforded him. "And we don't necessarily want to be the richest guys in the graveyard."

TIM BRABHAM

What's the best advice you've ever gotten?

Don't forget your failures or your challenges, but don't dwell on them either. Put them aside and keep going forward because you can't change the past, you can only learn from it and use it to influence your future decisions and actions.

If you were to receive an award, what would you want it to be for?

Being a good person and a well-rounded individual with varied interests.

Who or what inspires you?

My daughters and the unknown.

What do you see as the greatest challenge for the next generation of Americans?

Keeping up with the speed of change in the world, being able to filter the glut of information and break it up into actionable items.
More career choices, but less job stability.

What three (famous) people, living or dead, would you invite to your fantasy dinner party?

Albert Einstein
Leonardo da Vinci
Benjamin Franklin

Awareness isn't always about actively looking for the next opportunity; sometimes it's about marketing yourself so others become aware of who you are, what interests you, and what you have to offer. Tim Brabham has learned that showing genuine interest in others not only opens doors, but can sometimes bring opportunities right to your doorstep.

Just out of college in the early 1990s, Tim held various jobs at a couple of large U.S. companies before landing a position in 1993 at the headquarters of Janus Capital Group, the investment firm based in Denver, Colorado. "Back then, it was actually still a paper world and the company was just undergoing the change to electronic," shares Tim. "So I started out processing paperwork tied to transactions and the opening and closing of accounts." Within a short time, Tim began working directly with shareholders, opening accounts, processing transactions, and making fund recommendations based on investment goals. But about six months into it, he saw an opportunity for a better fit within the company.

"We were beginning a workforce management team to do the operations, forecasting, and planning for the call centers," describes Tim. "I mentioned to one of the executives that I would really like to go in that direction and be part of setting that up."

Expressing interest in going in a new direction paid off for Tim, as he became part of the small team responsible for Janus's call center operations. Over the next few years, Tim's career growth at Janus mirrored the company's rapid growth. "The company went from 450 people when I joined up to about 4,000 in the dot-com heyday," comments Tim. "While the company was growing, there was a lot of room for growth and I gradually expanded my scope of responsibilities."

In 1999, Tim began to feel that he had peaked within his area of specialty at Janus, and he quietly put out feelers for new employment opportunities at some of the telecommunications companies in the Denver area. "I was actually offered a position with one of the local telcos," recounts Tim. "But I turned it down because ultimately I felt like I had invested so much time at Janus that I wanted to try to continue to grow my career there."

He adds, "I was working for a company that, up to that point, had never had a reduction in workforce or contracted. It was growing rapidly along with the markets. So I decided that I wanted to stay safe and stay in my role. There was some loyalty, comfort, and job stability that I thought I would have by remaining there," he admits.

But with the economy soon in a sharp downturn, many companies could not sustain the pace of rapid growth they had enjoyed during the previous several years, and Janus was no exception. Says Tim, "Shortly after the bubble burst on the economy, Janus contracted from 4,000 heads down to about 1,800 heads over a course of six months." In the spring of 2001, Tim, an operations analyst at the time, became one of the casualties.

Married with two young daughters, Tim received what he calls a generous severance package from Janus, including outplacement services to help him find a new job. "I spent the next six months job hunting and spending time with the family," he recalls. "I was really trying to figure out what I wanted to do, and looking at the opportunities and also trying to figure out what I would do differently next go-round."

And he most assuredly discovered something significant that he would do differently in his next career move. With reflection, Tim became aware that what he had thought was loyalty to Janus had actually been complacency, and he made himself a promise. "I vowed that in the future, when I started topping out and running out of growth opportunities within a company, I would not make the mistake again of riding it out for too long and getting too comfortable within my role," explains Tim. "I decided I didn't want to be as personally invested in the company itself; that I needed to have some balance between my commitment to the company and the opportunities there."

Comfortably settled in Colorado, the Brabhams initially sought to stay in their community. "We were very happy where we were, with the climate, the house, and everything there," Tim remembers. "I did some job searching and had come across several opportunities, but they would've been a step backwards in terms of what I wanted to do career-wise and opportunity-wise. So I was hesitant to take any of those roles."

With little family in the area, Tim and his wife, Molly, began to talk enthusiastically about expanding the job search geographically, using the opportunity to relocate to a different part of the country where they would be closer to family and lifelong friends. "We pretty much made a spur-of-the-moment decision that we're undergoing change, there are no huge opportunities or anything to fit me here, so why don't we start looking nationwide to see if there's something that fits that would ideally get us closer to family," reports Tim.

Widening the geographical parameters of the job search proved fruitful. "As luck would have it, I stumbled across an opportunity that made Molly happy and made me happy relatively quickly," says Tim.

What caught his eye was a new position being created at Blue Cross of Rhode Island. The organization was looking to bring its call center operations from the paper world into the electronic world of the twenty-first century. "The company was going through the same sort of transition that we went through at Janus," describes Tim. Blue Cross was looking for someone knowledgeable about industry practices and the best way to establish an operations team, and Tim just happened to be heading to Rhode Island on vacation to visit some of Molly's family.

"I shot them an e-mail saying that I'm planning on being out there for vacation anyway and am interested in the role," recalls Tim. He met with the company and found that the opportunity was a win-win—a perfect fit. So in the fall of 2001, the family uprooted and moved to New England as Tim joined Blue Cross as their call center operations manager. "I got to leverage the skills that I had learned at Janus, and got pretty much free reign over creating an operations department myself," shares Tim. "I got a lot of autonomy and say-so on how things would be created and changes would be made within the organization. In an established company, I wouldn't have been given that opportunity."

Tim hired the operations team, put the software in place, designed the call routing, and changed the forecasting of scheduling and staffing plans for the operation. Because the organization was relatively small, he was also able to work on implementing customer relationship management projects, and design the voice menus through which customers would be routed.

While the job at Blue Cross was professionally rewarding, and Molly and the girls were gratified to be living close to family, Tim never stopped looking for new opportunities. "One of the things that I had told myself in the post-Janus days was that given the opportunity for something that made sense from a career perspective and for my family, I wouldn't be complacent and be hesitant to move on that again in the future," Tim emphasizes.

He kept in touch with several former Janus colleagues, and periodically reached out to one co-worker in particular, who had moved on to Dell in Austin, Texas. From time to time the two would share work challenges and bounce solutions off each other. "I'd have questions about things that I was trying to work through at Blue Cross and I'd give him a call and say, 'What do you think about X, Y, and Z? This is the type of stuff that I'm working on.' And we'd just kind of share stories, share experiences," says Tim.

Through these conversations, his friend at Dell became aware of the types of projects Tim was working on at Blue Cross, and apparently also sensed that Tim was open to new growth opportunities within the industry. "I guess he picked up on that," observes Tim. "Because one day I got a call saying, 'Hey, we've just had a new opportunity open up managing the relationship with all the outsource partners that we use for our call centers. We think you'd be a great fit for it. Do you want to fly out?'"

It was 2004, and after nearly three years at Blue Cross, Tim was starting to get antsy to return to a faster-paced, more quick-change environment like he had experienced at Janus, where there was more opportunity for advancement and expansion on his skill-set. So he flew to Austin to check out the job at Dell, and within a week, he had interviewed, been offered the position, accepted it, and was in the process of moving to Texas.

Tim says that Molly, ever supportive and flexible, had very little hesitancy about relocating for the opportunity, even though it meant leaving a part of the country where she had family and roots. "Yes, she was nervous about moving to a place where she essentially knew nobody—where we had no family, no friends, aside from the co-worker that thought I'd be a good fit for the position," admits Tim. "But she actually had mentioned that one of the things that she learned from moving to Rhode Island was that no matter where you move, you're going to find new friends, new people—it's a relatively easy thing to do."

Now with three daughters in tow, the Brabhams packed up and resettled in a completely unfamiliar part of the country. Tim credits the family's positive attitude for making the move an energizing adventure. "If Molly and I didn't have the same outlook and the same excitement around each of the moves, it would have been a much more difficult experience," observes Tim. "Were we both nervous about it both times? Of course, because both moves were huge commitments. It would be very easy to get mired in a negative mindset if you let yourself. But you've just got to look at the opportunity and push through it. I think Molly is an amazing person when it comes to being supportive from that aspect."

Almost six years later, the family is thriving in Austin. "The net positive for moving to Texas was a couple of different things," lists Tim. "Of course there was the job opportunity. Financially it was definitely beneficial—substantially more money in an area that's substantially less expensive from a cost-of-living standpoint. The climate is great, so we have a lot more time outdoors year-round, and the public school is head-and-shoulders better."

Tim continues to find growth opportunities at Dell. He joined the company as an outsource capacity manager, and has transitioned several times within the company to handle more complex global call center projects. In 2009, he was given responsibility for managing outsourcing service provider relationships for the consumer and small business organizations globally. In that role, he negotiates contracts with outsourcers for new product releases, and makes recommendations for support locations, staffing and compensation issues.

Says Tim, "Within Dell, the thing that has benefitted me has just been showing interest in other areas of the company." He continues, "I try not to look at just my piece of what I need to do. I'm the type of person who wants to understand how things work and why they work they way they do—why somebody makes a decision to implement a business strategy or why we designed a product in a specific way. And I think people pick up on that and when they have a need to bounce things off people, they tend to reach out to those people who show interest in their particular areas or are eager to learn other aspects."

Tim acknowledges that executives and colleagues have mentioned another appealing quality that makes him sought after within the company. "I've been told that people found it easy to share information and seek out my advice because the way I handle the business world is nothing personal, no politics," he notes. "Everything is around what's the right thing to do from a business standpoint. There is never really any agenda that I'm pushing."

Tim is acutely aware that in the business world, in addition to your verbal interactions, you're always sending subtle signals about who you are, what's important to you, and how your attitude influences your decisions and actions. Those signals have brought opportunity to Tim and his family, and he's grateful to have been able to take advantage of those circumstances to grow both professionally and personally. Looking back over his career to date, he advises, "If there's something that really interests you but you're nervous about doing it, take the chance. You never regret the chances that you took; you regret the chances you didn't take." Words to live by for any young—or even seasoned—professional.

4

REALISTIC VISION

"If you build it, he will come."
—*Field of Dreams*

DEAR BOYS,

Dreams have empowered humans since the beginning of time—guiding, inspiring, and enlightening people to develop workable theories, create solutions, and discover cures and answers. On its own, a dream is about as useful as a screen door on a submarine, but add soul-stirring passion and you've got a vision—an image of a future destination you ardently want to reach. With a vision firmly rooted in your heart and mind, you now stand at a pivotal crossroads. Launch headlong and headstrong down the first road you see, and you're eventually bound to discover that you've been cruising the boulevard of broken dreams. Instead, proceed inquisitively and judiciously. Take the time to study and investigate the market, and make an honest assessment of your strengths, abilities, resources, and the time required, because only when you confirm that your idea will fulfill a need, and that you've got access to the tools and resources necessary to achieve it, do you have a realistic vision worthy of pursuing.

A realistic vision is a beneficial springboard. It can serve as a powerful motivator and inspire unbridled creativity. But it then requires irrepressible energy, steely determination, gutsy courage, tireless industry, vibrant resilience, astute resourcefulness, self-modulated humility—and most importantly, a well-considered strategic plan—if you truly want a viable shot at bringing it to fruition.

Solid strategic planning will help ensure that you take small, reasonable steps rather than overextending your resources and putting your vision at risk. Your plan must be thoughtful and fluid, as well as flexible and adaptable to future challenges. Formulating it is but the first step; you continually need to revisit, reevaluate, and revise your plan, adjusting and refining as you proceed and learn. You must be willing and able to persist in the face of skepticism and rejection, focusing on overcoming obstacles and ignoring distractions along the way. But beware of having such resolute adherence to your own ideas and desires that you disregard overwhelming evidence that it's time to scrap your plan altogether.

One of the most invaluable gifts you can give yourself in evaluating and executing your vision—and in most other aspects of life as well—is to seek out and surround yourself with people you trust and respect, who are committed to giving you completely honest and constructive feedback. Ask those whose opinions and expertise you value to be part of your personal advisory group. Go to them for quality suggestions, reactions, and a reality check, and cultivate the feedback as a catalyst for growth. Sure, it can be difficult to hear the unadorned truth rather than gushing praise, but the only growth that comes out of constant accolades is the size of your ego. Listen to your advisors with the intent to absorb and thrive. Hear them out, and fully understand what's being shared without becoming defensive or dismissive. Take some time to process the feedback, and read between the lines to discern whether there's something glaring that's *not* being said. Remember, humility is the fine line between confidence and arrogance.

There's no better way to illustrate the difference between realistic vision and delusional dreams than to share "A Tale of Two Cousins." These two contrasting stories highlight the triumphs and pitfalls of pursuing an artistic vision.

The first story is about Dad's cousin, Dave Binder, and his career as a solo musical performer. Now in his 50s, Dave has been playing guitar since he was 7, writing songs since he was 10, and singing for as long as he can remember. Although he went off to college with a pre-med focus, he soon admitted that he wanted to study to become a professional musician. After earning a bachelor's degree in music, Dave took a risk and hit the road to take a shot at achieving his vision. Yet, he quickly found that playing gigs at clubs wasn't going to provide him with enough income to live the lifestyle to which he aspired.

Dave was also a proud advocate for his self-reliance—standing firm on his unwillingness to borrow money from someone else so he could follow his dream to be a musician. When he discovered that the college market was considerably more lucrative than the club circuit, he decided to create a show that would appeal to college students, incorporating other people's music into his act. According to Dave, another performer once asked him if he considered himself a sellout for not exclusively playing his own tunes. Dave replied, "At the end of every week, I go to the bank. Where do you go?"

A believer in taking things slow and smart, Dave regularly packed his equipment and his faithful companion, Pasha, a lovable Samoyed, into his van and drove from campus to campus, performing a variety of shows that he developed expressly for college crowds. He became a favorite with students, and his shows became annual traditions on a number of campuses. Dave remembers a popular colleague in the college market who figured that buying himself a plane would get him to gigs more quickly and allow him to bank more money. His friend suggested that Dave look into it, too. Satisfied with what he deemed the slower, smarter mode of transportation, Dave stuck with his reliable van, and says that by overextending himself with the expense of a plane, his friend wound up costing himself much of his profits.

In nearly 30 years of touring college campuses, Dave has played over 3,000 shows. He has released six musical projects, including three all-original CDs, and supplements his college gigs by playing corporate events and performing in the islands at Club Med. Even with his success, Dave continually reevaluates his business plan, making sure he is able to meet his goals of making a decent living and not owing money to anyone. He insists on testing the waters and listening to honest feedback before he invests his energy and talent into developing a new show. "I find out what the interest is before I go ahead," he explains. "For my James Taylor show, for example, I advertised and found out what the response was, and then I created the show."

While he's ever passionate about writing his own music and gets a kick out of having fans, in the end Dave views his music career as a business. "I knew that I'd have to sacrifice certain things in order to get other things," he reflects. "But the one thing I didn't want to give up was my security." By continually refining his vision to take advantage of opportunity, Dave has figured out how to maintain a successful enterprise by pursuing his dream.

The second story is about a cousin we'll call Denise. For this person's story, we'll keep the circumstances authentic but change the details to preserve anonymity. For 20 years, Denise ran a profitable therapeutic massage business while she dabbled as a jewelry designer in her spare time, fancying herself uniquely gifted. When she was in her late 40s, her father died, leaving her a six-figure trust fund and an extensive pre-Columbian artifact collection. Denise promptly decided to close up shop and sell off several pieces of art to fund a full-time jewelry venture. With enormous eagerness, she showed her designs to family and friends, leaving them little choice but to feel compelled to shower her with polite encouragement.

Denise was enthusiastic and aggressive about making connections with potential investors, buyers, and manufacturers, yet she constantly cast aside their less-than-lukewarm response to her work. Despite the discouraging feedback, she forged ahead, convinced that these successful industry experts were simply not enlightened enough to recognize her talent and vision. She sold her condo in New Hampshire and relocated to San Francisco to open a boutique, adding the equity from the condo sale to her inheritance and pursuing her dream.

Things didn't exactly take flight once Denise opened her jewelry shop, but she lived happily in a constant state of self-delusion. The occasional sale of one of her pieces gave her an increasingly inflated view of her talent, and she was fervent in her belief that she was the next big thing. When a longtime friend gently suggested that she reevaluate her plan, Denise became insulted and responded by jettisoning this person who didn't believe in her—essentially sticking her fingers in her ears and shouting, "La-la-la-la, I can't hear you!"

With no use for naysayers, Denise continued to surround herself exclusively with cheerleaders who nourished her insatiable appetite for praise. Ten years later, she has now blown through the entire proceeds of the trust fund, and income from the business has dried up to the point that she can no longer cover the rent on her small shop. Yet Denise still believes that through other channels she will become a resounding international success. She vows to exhaust every last penny to make it happen, even if it means resorting to selling off the balance of the artifact collection she inherited. She figures that in the unlikely case that fame and fortune isn't just around the next corner, she can always support herself by unfolding her massage table again.

If you draw any lesson from "The Tale of Two Cousins," let it be the importance of accepting reality and constructive criticism. Everyone makes mistakes and goes down the wrong path from time to time. The trick is to listen to honest feedback and cut your losses at some point rather than persisting on the road aimlessly and endlessly, in the hopes that something will change for the better. It's easier said than done, but sometimes it's wiser to abandon the sinking ship than to go down with the vessel and lose everything in the process.

One couple who turned their vision into a celebrated reality is Kate and Matt Jennings. In their profile you'll find out how two young entrepreneurs created the cheese shop and restaurant that serves your ultra-favorite comfort food, the most luscious and decadent version of macaroni and cheese on the planet. Their commitment to taking small steps and constantly refining their plan has enabled them to establish themselves as true visionaries, and has opened up opportunities that many only dream of. It's a delicious story that underscores the fact that there's no shortcut to success.

Keep your feet on the ground and keep reaching for the stars, Mama and Dad

KATE & MATT JENNINGS

What's the best advice you've ever gotten?

Laugh! And keep finding ways to laugh despite the situation.
Don't sacrifice quality.
Keep things small and manageable so you don't lose track of your original plan.

If you were to receive an award, what would you want it to be for?

Connecting people to the heritage of food.
Creating an approachable, unpretentious dining and shopping experience.

Who or what inspires you?

On a personal level, family.
On a professional level, the movement to take food seriously and become invested in the future of our food systems.

What do you see as the greatest challenge for the next generation of Americans?

Trying to get people to eat healthy and naturally regardless of economic status.

What three (famous) people, living or dead, would you invite to your fantasy dinner party?

Julia Child
Thelonious Monk
Dalai Lama

The tale of Kate and Matt Jennings is literally a cheesy love story.

The couple met as twentysomethings in 2000 at Formaggio Kitchen, the celebrated gourmet foods shop in Cambridge, Massachusetts. He worked as a cheese buyer, and she was the catering manager and baker, and they immediately realized they shared a passion for high-quality hand-crafted and fresh-grown food. Matt had received his culinary education at The New England Culinary Institute, and within a few months of their meeting, Kate made the decision to return to school for a formal education in baking. She was accepted to the accelerated baking program at the Culinary Institute of America (CIA) in St. Helena, California, and prepared to move clear across the country. Though they had been dating only six months, Matt ditched his plum position, which had sent him all over the globe in search of the world's best cheeses, and moved to the Napa Valley with Kate.

Both born and bred New Englanders, Matt and Kate considered the move temporary, planning to return to the East Coast in just over a year, when the CIA program ended. While Kate was fully immersed in her baking education, Matt got a job as the assistant wholesale manager for Cowgirl Creamery, an artisan cheesemaker and distributor based in Northern California.

"I was calling on all the Bay Area restaurants every week, talking cheese with them," he recounts. "Everybody from Thomas Keller to Farallon to Boulevard—all these incredible spots—talking to all these chefs and loving it."

But something was missing for Matt. "At heart I was really a retail guy. I missed the buzz of retail. I missed selling cheese and talking to people and getting customers excited and educating customers and all that stuff I had been doing at Formaggio," he recalls.

As Kate was finishing up the baking program, Cowgirl offered Matt an opportunity to move to San Francisco and return to retail. "They were going to open their new shop at Ferry Plaza, and the option was for me to take the job as the manager at the new shop or to head home to the east coast," he shares. The couple considered their future. "We were looking long-term, and we said, 'What is the reality?' The reality was buying a 1,000-square-foot home for $800,000 in Berkeley with a postage stamp yard, or we're going to move back east and be closer to family and have our dollars go a little further," says Matt. "So that's what we decided to do. We moved back."

They headed east with dreams in May of 2002. Matt was eager to open a retail cheese shop, and Kate couldn't wait to bake professionally.

Instead of returning to the Boston area, however, the couple decided to settle just south, in Rhode Island. "Matt's folks had retired in Little Compton," explains Kate. "I had never spent any time in Rhode Island, but we decided that we had been in Boston for years, so why don't we try something new. Originally we thought, 'Great, we'll move to Rhode Island, we'll try it out.' We didn't know if it was going to be forever."

Kate got her hands right into the flour, baking breads and pastries at Olga's Cup and Saucer, a beloved artisanal bakery in Providence, while Matt teamed up with a friend to develop a business plan for the cheese shop. He had a suspicion that the food scene that was starting to develop in Rhode Island might just be the right place to introduce the vision he had for his cheese shop.

"We had just gotten back from the west coast, where the idea of purchasing locally and buying everything from your produce to your meats from right around the corner and going to farmers markets was huge," describes Matt. "That whole food scene had just exploded in California. That was what we wanted to promote coming back to Rhode Island. We knew the concept had existed in New England a little bit," he continues, "but obviously not to the degree that it did in California, due to things like a longer growing season there. But we thought the concept could still be adaptable to New England—things like purchasing sustainably, supporting local farmers, all that sort of stuff."

Matt and his business partner envisioned a combination wine boutique and cheese shop that focused exclusively on artisanal American cheeses. But the partners immediately ran into a roadblock. "We quickly came to realize that Rhode Island state liquor laws would prevent us from selling alcohol if we were selling food, unless we were a restaurant," laments Matt. "The state doesn't allow side-by-side retail of liquor and food. So we kind of adapted a little bit. We said, 'We'll focus on the cheese shop and then down the road if we can get the liquor license, we'll do the wine shop next door.'"

The two business partners studied demographics and scoped out the state for nearly a year to locate a desirable spot in which to open their shop. They narrowed down their choices to the East Side of Providence—the state capital and home to Brown University, Johnson & Wales University and the Rhode Island School of Design—or the seaside city of Newport. "But Newport for us seemed a little too seasonal," confesses Matt. "So we focused on the East Side."

Matt looked around for space and continually came up empty. He and his partner wanted to buy, but couldn't find property they wanted to invest in. One day while hunting for real estate in Providence's Wayland Square, however, Matt stumbled upon a tiny establishment called The Cheese Shop of Providence. The shop had been in existence for about 50 years, and had been run for the last 20 by a husband-and-wife team. Matt says it was obvious at first sight that the couple had lost the love for their cheese business. "The place was totally unkempt, and I could see they were just kind of over it," he recalls.

So Matt made a proposal to the wife. "I just said to her, 'Hey, have you ever thought about selling?' And she said, 'No. This is a family business. I'm going to pass this on to my grandkids.' And I said, 'Okay.' And so we left and continued to look for other spaces. And she ended up calling me the next day, and she said, 'You know what? That actually might not sound so bad. So let's sit down and talk.'"

They met soon thereafter and had an honest conversation about assets, liabilities, and the established clientele and goodwill that the shop had cultivated within the neighborhood. Matt liked what he heard, and although the space was leased rather than owned, he and his partner bought the entity in the summer of 2003.

The little shop was tired, with old carpet that smelled like cigarette smoke, so the partners put in a tile floor and freshened up the space over the next few months. They expanded and upgraded the inventory, with a broad selection of gourmet items, dry goods, oils, pantry essentials, pâtés, terrines, and meats in addition to the domestic cheeses. They named the new shop Farmstead, and opened the doors just before Thanksgiving of that year to an appreciative community.

Shortly after opening, Matt realized he was going to have to bend a bit on his goal of exclusively carrying domestic cheeses. "Being in Providence, we had folks coming and wanting their parmesan and their provolone, and stuff like that. We realized that we would be stupid if we didn't listen to our customers," admits Matt. With a strong Italian-American population in the nearby Federal Hill section of the city, food products from Italy were not hard to come by, but high-quality edibles from other

European countries were noticeably unavailable in Providence. Farmstead began to fill the void by offering French, Swiss, and other imported cheeses and products. "We kind of latched on to that and offered some of those European specialties, but really wanted to make the point that our focus was artisan American. And it still is to this day."

The original intent was for Matt and Kate to eventually combine their culinary talents sometime down the road. "I wanted to pursue my baking at that time," explains Kate. "And Matt, obviously, was anxious to get the cheese shop up and running. We always figured we would be able to merge at some point."

But that point came sooner than they had both expected. Less than a year after opening Farmstead, Matt's original partner bailed. Acknowledges Kate, "That's basically when I said to Matt, 'I love baking, and I'll keep doing that part-time, but I'm going to jump on board with you and we'll do this together.'"

Although Matt was passionate about his vision to showcase domestic cheeses and artisan food products, the concept was fairly progressive for Providence in 2003. "A lot of people thought Matt was crazy, and didn't initially understand the concept of doing all the domestic cheeses," Kate confesses. "I think they just thought, you know, we're just new kids on the block and this is never going to fly."

But Providence was apparently ready for Farmstead, and soon Matt and Kate were so busy, they needed to hire their first employee, Victoria. "It was Matt, Victoria, and myself for a while," recounts Kate. "And then it just took off from there."

Amid the rush and madness of running a new operation, Matt knew it was time to make his relationship with Kate official on more than a business level. One night, she finished taking a shower and opened the curtain to find Matt kneeling on the bathmat, bearing an engagement ring, their two dogs next to him.

"He actually said, 'Will you marry *us*?' because obviously I wasn't just marrying him, we were starting a family with the two dogs as well!" laughs Kate. "We did everything backwards. We bought the house before we were married. We had the business before we were married." And so, in 2005, the two finally tied the knot.

Matt and Kate loved running their cheese shop, and Farmstead quickly caught on. Soon, enchanted customers began hinting that they wanted more. "People again and again were like, 'Oh, wouldn't it be great if you could just serve some wine and we could have a cheese bar here and you could expand on your sandwiches?'" remembers Kate.

The idea was particularly appealing to the young entrepreneurs, who figured they wouldn't even have to hire out to make it happen. Matt, who had worked as a chef earlier in his career, was missing cooking, and Kate was itching to get back to baking. "It got us thinking that if we could open a restaurant and start selling alcohol, that would help financially, which is obviously something you always have to look at," says Kate. And so the couple made the decision that if the small space next door to Farmstead ever opened up, they would give the concept a shot.

As luck would have it, the space soon became available, and Matt and Kate went for it. The original concept was for a small wine bar with cheeses and charcuterie from the shop, and light snacks. But once they started planning the 1,200-square-foot space, things changed. "We got in there and said, 'If we look at it from the perspective of needing to maximize our profit potential and trying to make as much per square foot as we possibly can—which from a business standpoint is kind of a no-brainer—then we're talking about doing more than wine and cheese,'" reveals Matt. "As we went into it, it just kind of grew."

Matt drafted a few menus and realized the concept had evolved into a full-scale restaurant. "I'm talking about getting a grill and doing fish and steaks and a burger and the best mac 'n cheese you ever had from all the cheeses that we sell in the shop," he recalls.

When La Laiterie at Farmstead opened in May of 2006, the intimate 34-seat restaurant was indeed grander than originally imagined. The European-inspired, New England bistro offered seasonal dishes created by hand, using fresh, quality ingredients sourced locally from sustainable farms and food producers. Whatever Matt and Kate couldn't get from those sources, they and their staff made themselves, including house-baked desserts, hand-cranked sausages, savory pâtés and condiments.

All their energy went into launching the new venture. "The first year and a half was absolutely crazy," recalls Kate. "Obviously all of our attention went to La Laiterie for a while because we were running the kitchen." As a practical matter, the couple had to entrust the running of the cheese shop to one of their employees. "It was a little strange to just hand it over to someone else. But in the same breath, we were figuring, 'Okay, Farmstead has been figured out and it's established. We need to put the attention into the new space,'" she adds.

La Laiterie was instantly embraced by the community, which recognized and appreciated unpretentious dishes made with a love for the craft of quality food. "I think what we were able to provide, almost by default, in the space that is La Laiterie, was kind of a small, cramped, SoHo-style, urban showcase for the best local food possible," says Matt. "It was something new and different for Providence, which has great bastions of Italian food and some cute and quaint French bistros, but nothing that I think is as warm and inviting and progressive and quality ingredient-driven as what we were doing at the time, and hopefully still continue to do," he adds.

Local and national media took note as well, and the bistro and cheese shop were featured with great acclaim in such publications as *Rhode Island Monthly, Food & Wine, Travel and Leisure, Bon Appétit,* and the *Wall Street Journal,* with Farmstead named to the *Saveur* 100 list in 2007.

Once La Laiterie was running smoothly, Matt and Kate saw another logical niche that they could serve: feeding the hungry business lunch crowd in the revitalized Downcity section of Providence. When a vacant space in the area became available in the spring of 2008, they jumped on the opportunity and opened Farmstead Downcity, specializing in gourmet sandwiches, soups, and salads to go.

The following year proved to be one of the most productive for the couple, both professionally and personally. That spring, Matt won the Boston leg of the Cochon 555 tour, a friendly competition in which five chefs are challenged to use a whole pig to create a series of dishes, with the goal of raising awareness of heritage breeds of pig in the culinary community. In the summer, the Farmstead crew prepared a five-course dinner for 180 people at a coastal farm in Portsmouth, Rhode Island, through Outstanding in the Field, an organization with a dual mission of reconnecting diners to the land and origins of their food, and honoring the local farmers and food artisans who cultivate it.

In September, life got even more thrilling with two long-awaited debuts. After closing for three months to embark on a thorough renovation, Farmstead's flagship location reopened, adding à la carte lunch service, a cheese bar, and a street-level temperature-controlled aging room for the 100 varieties of cheese available in the shop. And as if that was not enough excitement for the couple, Matt and Kate welcomed their first child, a baby boy named Sawyer, the very same week.

Kate instantly credits Matt as the visionary for the business they've created. "Matt's head is spinning all the time, to the point it's probably exhausting for him," she observes. "On a regular basis, he is always thinking about what's next. Not that he's not happy where we are," she continues, "but he's always thinking, 'Why don't we try this new idea, why don't we go out of the box, why don't we do one more thing.'"

Matt sees the success of the partnership a bit differently. "She's always been the brake, if you will, and I've always been the gas. And I think there's a lot to be said for coasting sometimes."

In order to achieve their dreams, Matt and Kate have realized that it's important to be able to step back from time to time and get a different perspective. As Matt says, "Part of taking that step back was finding some really strong, reliable people to put into key positions. Ultimately we make the final decisions, but we try to find people who are vested in what they do and interested in and passionate about what they're doing, and we work with them to promote the life of the restaurant and the shop." He continues, "We've been lucky enough to have found some great folks to help us hold it down."

The operation now employs 25, which gives Matt the opportunity to develop relationships with other socially conscious chefs and food purveyors. "Part of the process is letting go a little bit, and us being able to step back and look at the business as a whole, and do a lot more," he relates. "And so now we're able to do things like meet with the Rhode Island Farm Fresh Network, and help develop a mobile market system where chefs can go online and order local products and have them delivered to their door." He adds, "I can go now and work with the local pig farmer who has come to us because he wants to raise pigs for our restaurant. These are the dreams that you have as a cook."

In April of 2010, Matt again triumphed as the Boston winner of Cochon 555, extending his reign for a second year. He's also honored and excited to be preparing a dinner at the prestigious James Beard House in August of 2010, where, in keeping with his main focus, he's planning to interweave American artisan dairy products into each of the five courses he cooks.

Through it all, Matt aims to keep a realistic view of the volatile restaurant industry. "You never know when you're going to lose people, and I'll be right back in there working the line at night. But at the same time, you kind of have to latch onto these things when you have the opportunity," he concedes.

There are still a few elusive elements to the original vision that Matt and Kate would like to accomplish. "The one thing we would really like is to be able to sell the wine and the beer that we serve in the restaurant at a retail level," admits Kate. "Obviously we won't be able to do that in the state of Rhode Island. But sometimes we say that if we're crazy enough, maybe we'll do this concept again somewhere else."

Ultimately, Matt dreams of owning a space where he and Kate can create an environment of what he calls "pure gustatory excellence." It would include a retail shop for artisan food, wine and boutique beer, as well as a restaurant and an education center in which to hold culinary classes.

"I just thrive on bringing people together and celebrating the conviviality of what a great food experience can be," he explains. "Seeing that look across the counter in a customer's eyes when they suddenly understand what it is you're trying to explain to them, or seeing a little gleam in their eyes when they understand your passion for what you're doing—*that's* the best form of payment out there," he confides. "There is just a joy in doing what we do."

— 5 —

INTEGRITY &
POSITIVE
ATTITUDE

"How about a little piece of integrity
in this world that is so full of greed
and a lack of honorability that
I don't know what to tell my son!"
—Dorothy Boyd, in *Jerry Maguire*

HEY GUYS,

When Red Sox third baseman Mike Lowell was named Most Valuable Player of the 2007 World Series, you cheered even more wildly than when the final opposing batter had struck out moments before, giving the Sox the title of World Champions. Indeed a talented hitter and scrappy infielder, there was something far beyond Lowell's athletic prowess that you recognized and admired. You saw him play with heart, humility, and an unrelenting respect for the game every day. He seemed to give off a positive vibe on and off the field, and was continually praised by his teammates for his professionalism and leadership in the clubhouse, crossing racial and cultural lines. You read about his dedication as a father, his gratitude as a son, his strong belief in faith, his determination to beat testicular cancer, and his remarkable pride in his Cuban heritage. At the time, you were a bit too young to be able to articulate just what seemed to make this man so special, aside from his baseball skills. Well, boys, that intangible attribute you admired so greatly is called integrity.

Integrity is the quality that locks in your core convictions and causes you to live consistent with them, like a personal code of honor. Having integrity requires establishing a strongly held set of beliefs, and basing your decisions and choices on those values and principles.

Actions unmistakably speak louder than words, and everything you do is a reflection of your capacity for integrity. Whether you keep your word and fulfill your commitments. Whether you choose to do the right thing when no one's looking. How you value honesty and truthfulness. Whether you're willing to accept blame or admit when you're wrong. How you perform. How you treat people. Whether you're able to keep information in confidence.

You will be bombarded almost every day with circumstances that tempt you to stray from your principles, and your response will reveal the fortitude of your integrity. Some instances may be blatantly illegal and unethical, like being offered a bribe in an attempt to influence your decision or opinion. Others may be subtler and more easily rationalized, like supporting someone disingenuously, just because of what that person may be able to do for you. Silly as it may sound, consider the range of timeless moral and ethical dilemmas faced by the Brady kids throughout five seasons of *The Brady Bunch*. Through the miracle of syndication, these six fictional characters are destined (or perhaps doomed?) to have their integrity tested in perpetuity.

- Think about Marcia, who has to decide whether to break a date with nice-guy Charley when hunky Doug Simpson—"big man on campus"—asks her to the dance, as well. Is it okay to tell someone to whom you've made a commitment that "something suddenly came up" when you're subsequently offered a better or more appealing opportunity?
- What about when Greg is grounded from driving, yet borrows a friend's car to go to a concert and insists that his parents' exact words were that he was only restricted from driving the family car? Is it right to breach or exploit the spirit of an agreement for your own benefit?

- How about when Cindy becomes a tattletale and squeals on her siblings—and even shares seemingly damaging information about Alice and the postman with Alice's boyfriend, Sam? Do you feel a duty to be discreet with private or confidential information that you've been asked or expected to keep secret?

- Or when Bobby lies boastfully to his friends, claiming to know football star Joe Namath, and then pretends to be gravely ill so Mr. Namath will pay him a visit? Is it right to intentionally mislead someone to save face or for your personal gain?

- What about when Peter breaks a vase—even though Mom always said, "Don't play ball in the house"—and his siblings take the blame for him so he doesn't jeopardize his camping trip? Should you ever let others accept culpability for your blunders? Is it ever right to cover for a friend or colleague, or look the other way when someone has clearly done something wrong?

- Remember the infamous "Marcia, Marcia, Marcia!" episode, where Jan, tired of living in her older sister's shadow, is determined to achieve something Marcia never has? Jan is thrilled when she wins first prize in an essay contest, but soon discovers that there's been a mistake in the scoring. Is it actually cheating when it's someone else's error? Is it ever okay to cheat?

The way you handle situations like these speaks volumes about your integrity. Following your moral compass faithfully and consistently takes tremendous discipline and strength, and upholding your beliefs in the face of negative influences is even more challenging. When you're being urged to compromise your values by conforming to peer pressure or popular opinion, you will need to muster every ounce of self-confidence you possess to stay true to your convictions. Take the opportunity to hear the rationale and reason being presented to you, but ultimately listen intently to your conscience. Resist the temptation to go with the flow or adopt the popular mindset just because it's what the crowd is doing; instead, have the self-assurance and conviction to hold your moral ground and do what you believe is right.

Young children often have an abundance of self-confidence, but with an accumulation of negative life circumstances and experiences, it's easy for that spirit to dissipate. Approaching life with a positive attitude is immeasurably beneficial to developing a robust sense of self-confidence. Your attitude is entirely your responsibility and exclusively within your control. Having a positive attitude helps you see possibilities as opposed to limitations and obstacles, and boosts you to cope more competently and comfortably with your daily activities. It inspires motivation, persistence, and tenacity, and stimulates you to think constructively to surmount challenges.

Being negative is draining, and it effectively repels people. Think of Debbie Downer, the fictional character from *Saturday Night Live*, who dampens the mood of everyone around her as she reports negative news and delivers pessimistic pronouncements. There will always be people who constantly find the negative in life, but there's no reason why you have to ascribe to their worldview. Negativity breeds negativity. But fortunately, positivity is contagious as well. Keep the Debbie Downers at arm's length, and surround yourself with upbeat optimists, people who encourage you, people who make you laugh, people who are kind and sunny and have an abundant zest for life.

It's also advantageous to take a forward view, rather than dwelling on past failures or wallowing in self-pity. Spend time productively, making positive changes and finding solutions, rather than dragging yourself down further by continually whining and complaining. Look for the bright side or the silver lining, and appreciate those blessings. Don't just see the proverbial glass as half-full; see a sparkling, hand-crafted crystal flute bubbling with the finest, most elegant champagne, or a classic soda fountain glass filled to the midpoint with a rich, frosty chocolate milkshake—or whatever happens to tickle your fancy.

Sure, "stuff" happens. Sometimes it's difficult, life-changing stuff. If it's a situation you can impact, make the choice to take action and affect the most positive possible outcome. Choosing to spend time worrying about circumstances that you can't impact or control is, frankly, futile, and progressively depressing. Worrying won't change the outcome, it will only sap joy out of the present. Instead, anticipate the realistic repercussions of the worst-case scenario, and prepare yourself as thoroughly as possible—emotionally, physically, spiritually, financially—to accept them if they indeed become actuality. Then explore all feasible means of avoiding the worst-case scenario. That way, if the worst case ultimately comes to pass, you won't be caught off guard, feeling shell-shocked and too paralyzed to handle the situation. And if you do wind up dodging a bullet and circumstances aren't as dire as you had mentally planned for, you can genuinely appreciate your good fortune and breathe a grateful sigh a relief. However, if you routinely plan for only the most favorable outcomes and fail to prepare yourself for the potential reality of more adverse circumstances, you could find yourself spending a lot of time feeling disappointed, frustrated, and perpetually stressed.

Make it your trademark to greet people with enthusiasm, and you'll radiate positive energy and create a positive environment wherever you go. Can you guess one of the simplest, yet most powerful tools to spread a positive attitude? A smile! Smile when you speak to someone in person or on the phone. Even though the person on the opposite end of the phone can't see your smiling face, it adds a dash of effervescence to your voice that will often favorably change the demeanor of the person you're talking to. That makes the seemingly insignificant act of smiling doubly powerful—it gives you a lift and it just might momentarily brighten up the recipient's day.

Although their lives are vastly dissimilar, the two people we've chosen to profile in this chapter share a strong moral resolution and an optimistic energy for moving forward. Ellis Waldman and his family have known Mom's family for generations. A business owner and community leader, Ellis is never without a warm smile and a considerate word, and his willingness to champion causes and projects he earnestly believes in—regardless of prevailing opinions—has earned him immense respect and admiration among friends, colleagues, and community members.

In addition, we feature the poignant story of Marucha Andrzejewski, whom we have befriended through rewardingly genial visits to her tailor shop in Southport, Connecticut. Marucha literally had to move forward and not look back when she was evacuated to the United States in 1962 from her homeland of Cuba, amid escalating international tensions. Profoundly grateful for the personal freedoms she has been afforded in her new country, Marucha worries that the more removed Americans become from the immigrant experience, the more we will take these sacred freedoms for granted. Both of these people abound with integrity, kindness and, character.

Catch ya 'round,
Mama and Dad

ELLIS WALDMAN

What's the best advice you've ever gotten?

The only thing you have is your name: Don't destroy it.
Define yourself and be yourself.

If you were to receive an award, what would you want it to be for?

I wouldn't want to receive an award. What would mean more to me would be to be remembered for the gift of touching someone's life and having theirs touch mine.

Who or what inspires you?

Opportunity and improvement.

What do you see as the greatest challenge for the next generation of Americans?

How to relate to people beyond electrons.
Education isn't enough.
Entitlements are gone.

What three (famous) people, living or dead, would you invite to your fantasy dinner party?

John F. Kennedy
Roger Williams
Dr. Martin Luther King, Jr.

LEADING WITH INTEGRITY

If you mixed together equal parts integrity, determination, and humility, and topped it with a heaping dollop of kindness, you would come pretty close to the recipe for a gentleman named Ellis Waldman. And it's largely because of Ellis's remarkable sense of passion and compassion that the company his father established nearly 80 years ago remains one of the largest automation engineering and industrial service companies in the country.

As far back as he can remember, Ellis has had a "can-do" attitude toward issues and projects he vigorously believes in. "I'd say that it's the way I'm wired," he suggests. "I think it's the circuitry. It's the DNA. It's the way I've always been." While he acknowledges some bumps along the way that dampened his spirit, Ellis has almost always approached life with bold determination and a heartfelt appreciation for people—making him a valued community leader as well as a respected business owner.

Ellis's father, Edmund Waldman, founded Walco in Providence, Rhode Island, in 1931 as a manufacturer and seller of radio antenna kits. The company soon saw an opportunity in repairing and rebuilding electric motors used in the region's heavily concentrated wire and textile industry. Over the next four decades, as the region and the bustling Port of Providence grew, so did the company. Walco eventually became one of the largest electrical apparatus service facilities in the northeast.

Growing up the third of four children, Ellis treasured his close relationship with his dad. "He was building the business. I remember going through school, even through high school, he'd come back at 10:00, 10:30 at night. He might take us to school, but he'd be home late," he shares. "I would often go down and sit at the kitchen table with my mom when she made tea for him when he came in. And I'd long for the Saturdays when he'd come in to work and I could come in with him. I had a chance to be with him. So we were very close, and that connected me with the company."

During his school years in the late 1950s and early 1960s, Ellis worked summers in the family business. He remembers how busy the operations were during those years. "There was never a case of, 'How do we get business in?' It was only a case of, 'How do we get it out?'" he recalls. "We would be working July 4th, weekends, around the clock. I can't tell you how many times I'd be here in the shop for 24, 36 hours with other people."

Ellis joined Walco full-time in 1969, after finishing graduate school and active military duty. His sheer determination made an immediate impression on one of the company's longtime operations managers, who Ellis remembers saying to him, "You know, you don't give up. I think if you were on one side of a cinderblock wall and you had to get to the other, you'd use your head back-and-forth to burrow a hole!"

But Ellis quickly discovered that the business environment had changed since those busy summers he had spent working in the shop. Textile manufacturers had left the area, significantly reducing Walco's customer base. Family politics surfaced. The rosy career Ellis had been envisioning since childhood just wasn't there. "Those things didn't change *me*, because I guess to the core we are who we are, but it made things very difficult, made things very hard," recalls Ellis.

Further weighing on him was the fact that shortly after he joined the company, both of his parents began to experience deteriorating health. "When I came back here," he says, "my dad was out more than he was in. He was not well. And then my mom started to get sick. And all of these things at once—it was like somebody turned life upside down on me. It took a while for me to kind of be able to gather myself and get above sea level," he explains.

It wasn't until after his father passed away in 1984 that Ellis finally had to rise to the challenge of running Walco. "When my dad passed away, I really went under. That was hard for me. I was really under water emotionally," he shares.

Searching for internal strength after such an emotionally devastating loss, Ellis reflected on one of the most profound pieces of advice he ever remembers receiving. "I don't even know who it was," he admits, "But I remember someone told me one of the greatest lessons they learned is that you have to be yourself, you have to define yourself, you have to own yourself. That's when a lot of things started to come together within me and change."

To Ellis, defining himself meant getting back in touch with that unrelenting doggedness.

He strove to find a way to make the family business thrive again, not only out of respect to the memory of his father, but to keep Walco's workers employed so they could provide for their own families. Because there was so little industrial business left in the area, Ellis was going to have to look beyond the usual industries to uncover innovative opportunities. He would need to find niche markets that would sustain Walco and utilize the skill sets it had developed.

He put into practice the advice he had gotten about being himself, defining himself, owning himself—and it gave him the confidence to bid contracts in new areas, including mass transit. "We got into fixing the motors that are underneath mass transit type of rail cars like Metro North, New York Transit Authority underground, MBTA in Boston. And there's a whole world of equipment beneath there," he says. The mass transit industry became a key market for Walco, and today the company has contracts with rail companies as far south as Washington, DC, and as far west as Ohio.

The mass transit business led Walco into another niche market: fixing traction motors on freight diesel locomotives. Walco's high-tech automation business focuses heavily on the metals processing industry, and through a job with a customer in Mexico, Ellis made excellent contacts that prompted him to open an office in Monterrey, the heart of Mexico's steel industry. The company's workers learned how to work on larger pieces of equipment, and now they repair motors from power generation stations as far away as Pennsylvania, New York, New Jersey, New Hampshire, and Maine.

"Finding those kinds of niches, being opportunistic, that's what we've been able to do," offers Ellis. "And I think from that, we gained some confidence about how and where to grow, and what other areas to move into. If we didn't do that, I think we would have withered away."

Although his leadership has guided the company to expand in new directions, Ellis sees Walco's nearly 100 employees as the company's most valuable asset. "I have always appreciated that the employees are the company. They really are," he insists. While he believes it's foolish for any business leader to treat employees with anything other than respect, Ellis goes far beyond to champion a culture of sensitivity and empathy for the people who make up Walco's workforce.

"These people come here every day, and they have a lot of things going on in their lives," he explains. "They have medical issues. They have marital issues. They have parental issues. They have children's issues. They have all the things that exist in life. So they're dealing with all of those things, and to some extent they have to kind of park them at the doorstep and come in and do a day's work."

He goes on, "A leader can set a vision, but as a leader you have to be able to bring along the people you're leading to see that vision. You have to know where they're coming from—where they're starting from—and treat them with respect." Ellis's conviction that people value purposefulness comes through resoundingly. "People really want to feel like they're contributing. They don't want to feel like they're just taking a free ride. And what we do here is I believe we treat them with the utmost respect."

Since taking the reins of the company, Ellis has established guidelines for promoting a compassionate workplace. First and foremost, there is a zero tolerance policy for ethnic or sexual insults, and name-calling is strictly forbidden. "I don't care if you've been here 30 years, that doesn't go," he stresses. "We can use a four-letter word toward a job—you know, 'this freakin' job'—but not 'freakin' Joe.'" When he first implemented the policy, he says there was a lot of testing. "But when you take somebody who's been here 25 or more years and say, 'Sorry, you have a three-day suspension. We're not doing that here,' the rest don't do it again."

While by his account Walco was a compassionate company before he arrived, he acknowledges that years ago management sometimes turned a blind eye to offensive behavior. "I simply can't do that," insists Ellis. "Some years ago, we had a supervisor out there and he was doing things that weren't right. And even though customers liked him, he was doing things that weren't right and I terminated him. It cost us a chunk of business. And I'd do it again, because I think if I didn't do that and I stood up in front of these people, as I do many times during the course of the year, they'd just kind of look and laugh."

Above all, Ellis treats his workers with dignity. "Sometimes people get in trouble and they need some help, and we'll help them. And we do it without saying anything."

Personal conviction has always been one of Ellis's hallmarks, both in the business world and in life. "If there's something that's important and that I believe in, I'm not going to stop." He adds, "I think if you believe in something and are determined, there will be a way to accomplish it."

One issue that has long touched Ellis's heart is the care of Rhode Island's elderly Jewish population. When Providence's Jewish Home for the Aged was closed in the early 1990s amid community strife, Ellis found himself under tremendous pressure as acting president of the organization. Other community leaders and organizations abandoned the nursing home, but Ellis stood strong.

"People were yelling at me, nobody would stay next to me because they didn't want to be connected to the Jewish Home," he recounts. "But I had talked with a lot of people and it was apparent that there was still a need for a place to care for our elderly. There were lots of needs."

Despite negative opinions among the local Jewish community about the need for a Jewish assisted living residence, Ellis's committed leadership and heartfelt dedication was instrumental in the planning, fundraising, and construction of the Phyllis Siperstein Tamarisk Assisted Living Residence, an elegant 66-unit facility with personalized care, including a memory support wing. The facility has been occupied to capacity since it opened in 2003, with a constant waiting list ever since. Ellis says it wasn't intelligence or wisdom that led him to persist in his vision for Jewish eldercare. "It was emotion and determination, both from within," he confides.

Although his leadership and opinions are widely valued by community organizations, Ellis makes it a point to commit his support only to projects and issues that are personally and professionally meaningful. "I don't do things to prove something to anybody else; it's what's important to me," he shares.

A prime example was his decision to join a group of neighboring businesses and organizations that have joined forces as the Providence Working Waterfront Alliance. The group believes that the Port of Providence, where Walco is located, is a vital regional economic resource that must be protected from mixed uses that are incompatible with a working waterfront. They are taking a united stand against the City of Providence by promoting the continued industrial use of the waterfront, and consequently, preserving hundreds of well-paying blue-collar jobs in the area. When a lifelong acquaintance approached him about joining the Providence Working Waterfront Alliance, Ellis did not mindlessly jump on board because of their longtime relationship; he took some time to consider the purpose and goals of the organization. While Walco's existence does not depend on waterfront access, and selling the facility to a residential developer could be lucrative, Ellis ultimately decided on principle to join his industrial waterfront neighbors. "I thought about it and said, 'You know, it just doesn't make any sense to do what the city is doing. It makes no sense. It's wrong for the city. It's wrong for the people in the city. Where else are they going to get jobs like these?'"

When dealing with potentially contentious issues, part of Ellis's intrinsic diplomacy stems from his belief in the concept of multiple realities. "Someone once taught me the concept, and it's been a great lesson for me," he discloses. "It's really a fairly simple concept. You and I might see things from different perspectives, and when you think about it, each of us is right," he explains. "You see something from one way, and I see it from another, and that becomes our reality. You have to understand it's not like somebody else is wrong—it's just you have a belief in a certain direction." Keeping that concept in mind allows Ellis to keep things from going in a negative direction. "I'll try and look at that, and I won't set off and blow my stack at somebody," he notes, adding, "But in the end if I decide something's important to me, that's what I'm going to do. I will find a way."

In addition to being able to consider multiple realities and affording personal respect, Ellis calls humility an integral component of effective leadership. "If you don't have those three things, then you really can't be a leader," he maintains. "It's one thing to have a positive attitude, as long as it's tempered with humility."

Over the last 10 years, Ellis has focused his keen and passionate determination on the development of what he believes is a groundbreaking piece of industrial equipment called the Dolphin. Named because it was originally based on acoustic engineering, the Dolphin is a highly accurate non-contact electromagnetic gauge that continually measures the thickness of metals being used in industrial applications. When he describes the invention, his eyes light up and he is as proud as a first-time father. "It's been almost 10 years in the making, so talk about determination!" he proclaims. "I can remember a couple different times when my chief technology guy in this came to me and said, 'Ellis, we've got a problem and I just don't think it's possible,'" he confesses. "Well, when you have the kind of skin in the game that I do on this, I can't accept that. It's got to be possible. Bumblebees aren't supposed to fly." He vows to march onward. "We're going to find a way," he insists.

But even if the Dolphin gauge is a resounding success, Ellis has different aspirations for his eventual legacy. "Even if we're successful with this device, in 10 years nobody is going to know where that Dolphin gauge came from," he shares. "So whether it's my time this afternoon or 10 years or 20 years from this afternoon, if I can with an open heart be meaningful to my wife, Debbie, and my daughter, Edie, and maybe a couple other people—if I can touch someone's life and have them touch mine—that's the gift. That's all I want. I don't know what else I could do in life that would be more meaningful."

Ask almost anyone who has the honor and pleasure of knowing Ellis, and they will tell you that with the sincere prayer that he reaches ripe old age, he's already accomplished his hope—many times over.

MARUCHA ANDRZEJEWSKI

What's the best advice you've ever gotten?

Don't look back.

If you were to receive an award, what would you want it to be for?

Being a good wife, mother, and grandmother.

Who or what inspires you?

My faith.

What do you see as the greatest challenge for the next generation of Americans?

Keeping secularism from diluting integrity, morals, and faith.

What three (famous) people, living or dead, would you invite to your fantasy dinner party?

Jesus Christ
St. Theresa of Ávila
My father

LOOKING FORWARD, MOVING FORWARD

There are only two viable options from which to choose when you encounter unexpected change in your life. You can live stagnantly and delude yourself into believing that things will revert to their previous state, or you can embrace reality and summon the strength and faith to move forward. Marucha Andrzejewski chose the latter, and discovered the inimitable blessing of freedom.

Marucha was born into an educated, middle-class family in Guantánamo, Cuba, in the early 1940s. Her father was an accountant and university professor, and her mother, whom she lovingly describes as a regal and stylish woman, was an entrepreneur who ran a small business. The couple owned a home and a beach hut, and sent Marucha and her three siblings to private schools. Marucha describes that it was common for middle-class families to have domestic help. "We were not wealthy, but we were comfortable," she notes. "We had maids and we had a nanny, but they were not like they are here in America."

Eventually her parents divorced, and her mother remarried an American civil service worker who commuted from their home in Guantánamo City to his job at the military base at Guantánamo Bay. When the relationship between the United States and Cuba broke down in 1960, Marucha's mother, stepfather, and younger brother had to move to the base. Marucha remained with her father in the city but made frequent visits to her family at Guantánamo Bay.

One Saturday, Marucha's mother asked her to do a favor and escort an elderly friend named Emilio to the base, as they were afraid he would get lost on the way if he came on his own. Marucha was not particularly enthusiastic about spending a Saturday traveling with an older gentleman, but she reluctantly agreed. When the two arrived at the base, an American Marine checked their passports at the gate, and soon Marucha became aware that the Marine was admiring her. "This guy was winking at me," she recalls. "I was mad because I didn't want to be there. It was Saturday. I didn't want to be with Emilio." She continues, "And this guy started winking at me and getting closer and closer. I said he better not come any closer because I wasn't in the mood to be social."

Marucha stayed with her parents at the base for the weekend, and once she got back to the city, she found herself busy with exams. It was six weeks before she returned to the base, and in the meantime the policy on the base had changed, no longer permitting access by car, so she arrived by bus. "I was sitting on the bus and I looked down, and there he was again, the one that was winking and all that stuff," recounts Marucha. "And he looked up and he said, 'I have to see you!'" Marucha knew her stepfather did not welcome military personnel at their home. "I was bringing these beautiful tangerines to my mom and I felt bad for the Marine," she confides. "So I said, 'Here. A consolation prize.' I felt bad."

That evening, as she was getting ready to go back home to the city, the doorbell rang at her mother and stepfather's house. Marucha opened the door to find the Marine standing there. She began to tell him that she couldn't see him, when her stepfather— a tall, imposing fellow—told her to let him in. The Marine introduced himself as Richard, and asked for her stepdad's permission to visit Marucha. While Richard spoke to her parents in the living room, Marucha sat in the dining room and listened in on the conversation. Knowing her stepdad, she expected that Richard would be out the door within 10 minutes. But she soon became impressed with the way he handled her parents. "He was just very together," reports Marucha. "After two hours he was there, I said,

'I like this boy.' Because he wasn't intimidated. He handled the situation, and that's when I liked him and that was it."

Marucha and Richard quickly fell in love and intended to marry, but it was important to Marucha that her father give them his blessing before they entered into this union. It took nearly two years to convince him. "My father didn't want the marriage to happen because that means I would have to come to the United States," reveals Marucha. "And my father didn't want to separate the family. He was a wonderful dad. He is my hero. But Richard says he'll stay there. He embraced the Cuban culture." In July of 1962, Marucha was 19 years old when she and Richard were married in Puerto Rico.

Richard was immediately deployed to the Mediterranean, and Marucha got a job as a computer programmer on the base. "We thought the Castro situation was a temporary thing," she says. "Richard was going to come back to Cuba and he already had a job offer. So this was our plan. We were going to stay there, in Cuba."

One Sunday night several months later, however, Marucha heard the sound of planes flying over her house. "I didn't know what was going on. All night, you could hear planes flying and we lived far from the airport, but you could hear."

When she went to work the next morning, her boss immediately sent her home, instructing her to pack a small bag of necessities. "He said, 'We'll pick you up. You're leaving.' But I thought it was a drill, which we had in the past."

There were several American cruise ships in the Caribbean, and they were redirected to the base. Marucha, her mother, and younger brother boarded the cruise ship. Her mother was also convinced it was a drill, insisting they would be off the boat within a couple of hours. "But when the ship started moving, I figured this was real," recalls Marucha. "And it was terrible because I never had a chance to say goodbye to my dad. It was sad." She continues, "We have gorgeous mountains where I come from, and I see them leaving behind. I said, 'Oh, when am I going to see these again?'"

The ship landed at the military base in Norfolk, Virginia. Because it had been a rush to leave the country, no one who made the journey had packed more than the bare necessities. Upon arrival, the evacuees were taken to warehouses filled with used clothing that they could pick through. "We went there, and I see my mother, with this air about her, digging for clothes for us," shares Marucha. "She made a pile. A coat, which I never wear a coat in Cuba. But it was Virginia. It was late October. It was cold."

She goes on, "A coat, a couple of outfits. She folded them, and she gave them to me and she must have read my face. She looked at me and she goes, 'We are not looking back. We had what we had in our life over there. We're here now. Forward.'" Marucha can still picture her heretofore glamorous mother on her knees, digging for clothes as she advised her daughter to focus on the future rather than dwell on the past. Marucha understood, and took her mother's words to heart.

Her husband had told her that if something happened and she found herself in the United States, she should go to Connecticut to be with his family until he returned from duty. Marucha moved in with her husband's married sister, who was her same age. Her mother and younger brother settled in Virginia, where her stepfather eventually joined them.

Her father, however, was not allowed to leave Cuba. "I finally got in touch with him," discloses Marucha. "And he said, 'Don't worry about it. You know how these governments are. You'll be back here within two years.'" Stripped of all his assets by the government in an effort to redistribute wealth, Marucha's father had to survive by depending on the kindness of relatives and waiting for an occasional covert contact to bring money from family in the United States.

American life was shocking to Marucha. "My husband was away, and we were in a new culture, which was a shock to me." Watching *The Ed Sullivan Show* on television with her sister-in-law one night was one of the most eye-opening experiences for Marucha. On the show was a comedian whose routine included a less-than-flattering impression of President Kennedy. Marucha's sister-in-law and her husband were laughing riotously at the comic, while Marucha sat horrified.

"I said, 'How could you laugh at this guy who is going to be killed as soon as he leaves the studio?' And she said to me, 'Not here,'" remembers Marucha. She pressed her sister-in-law further. "I said, 'You mean to tell me you could be critical of the president and nothing happens? You could write whatever you want in a newspaper? I could go on a corner and yell, 'I hate this president!' and it's all good?'"

"Yes," her sister-in-law explained. "We have freedom of speech."

Marucha was overwhelmed. "To me, it was the best thing. It was delicious when she told me that." Her chilling experience in Cuba had been that people were summarily killed for protesting or speaking out against the revolution. "During Batista and Castro, I lost some of my friends that were underground fighting for the dictatorship," she reveals. She would sometimes go to school and see empty seats, and when she got home, her mother would tell her they needed to pay respects to the family of the missing students because they had been killed for expressing dissention.

Life could not have been more different in her new country, and Marucha savored her newfound freedom. She welcomed her husband home to Connecticut in March of 1963, and Richard soon found a job working for a paint contractor. The following month, the couple welcomed their first child, a daughter. Two more daughters and a son arrived in rapid succession over the next four years. Marucha, who had been a computer programmer in Cuba, took a job as a keypunch operator and verifier at a bank, working the night shift so she could take care of her children during the day.

Marucha constantly longed for her father to be able to meet her children, and he never lost his conviction that someday the family would indeed be reunited. In 1966, her father was at last able to leave Cuba under a newly enacted law that enabled Cuban citizens to be claimed by children under the age of 18 living in another country. Marucha's younger brother, who had left Cuba with her four years earlier, claimed their father. At 65, he was suffering with illness when he arrived in the United States.

Marucha and her husband were both employed—Richard had gone out on his own and started a paint contracting business— and they were about to build a new home for themselves in a Connecticut suburb. They planned for her father to move in with them, and were happy to have the opportunity to care for him in his retirement. Her dad went to church in his new community, where he was told that he qualified for welfare. But he made it clear to Marucha that he wasn't willing to take it.

"I said, 'That's great. You don't have to. We are working,'" shares Marucha. The following day, her dad went out for a long walk, and when he came back, he announced that he had gotten a job. Marucha asked what he would be doing, and he told her he would be working in a factory, gluing chairs. Marucha was heartbroken, picturing her proud, educated father, who had been a professional in Cuba, gluing chairs in a factory.

"I said to him, 'No, you are not. I'll get longer hours. You are not going to do this. You are not going to glue chairs,' and he said, 'Yes, I am,'" Marucha recounts. "He goes, 'You know, Maru, that's your problem. I don't have a problem gluing chairs.' And he went and worked.'"

Her father was fortunate to meet four of the couple's six eventual children before he passed away early in 1968. "My fear was that he would die in Cuba and I would not see him," confides a tearful Marucha. "But he had such a strong faith. He goes, 'You know, the Lord is not going to let me die until I see you and my grandchildren.' And I believed him. And the Lord delivered."

Shortly thereafter, Marucha decided to stay home full-time. "To me, it was the best job," she says of raising her children, finding joy in cooking, sharing family meals, and sewing clothes for her brood. "I'm thankful to be here in this country," she insists. "I realize what I didn't have back there—not the material things, but the freedom that my children were born with here so I didn't have to worry about them dragging them out and killing them in front of me." She goes on, "I appreciate this country. I love it more than a lot of Americans that were born here."

There will always be a tiny piece of Marucha's heart that longs wistfully for the beautiful life she remembers as a young girl in Cuba. "This is my home, but there is not a day that I don't think about either the music or my childhood, which was fantastic," she offers. She savors sweet memories of the majestic mountains and visiting her beach cottage in a little fishing village and digging for hidden treasures rumored to have been stashed by pirates in nearby caves. She recalls the intoxicating scent of gardenias that wafted in from a bush outside her bedroom window as she drifted off to sleep every night. "It is wonderful opportunity that this country offered us, but deep down, it's a longing," she laments.

After her children finished their education, Marucha and her eldest daughter opened a tailoring business, a tiny shop that's always filled with music and warm laughter. Marucha proudly shows off pictures of her seven grandchildren, including her 20-year-old grandson, a cadet at West Point. Although he is unsure where he will be stationed for military service, one possibility is Cuba, and he tells his grandmother he will become a SEAL and liberate the country. Marucha says there is nothing he could do that would make her any prouder of him than she already is.

And as for the handsome, amorous Marine who was instantly smitten by the pretty teenager as she arrived at the base at Guantánamo Bay more than 50 years ago? A loving smile spreads across Richard's face as he talks about his bride. "She is as beautiful today as she was the first day I saw her."

"It's been wonderful," Marucha reflects. "Let me tell you, I'm blessed. All this country is blessed."

— 6 —

RESILIENCE & ACCOUNTABILITY

"Just keep swimming.
Just keep swimming.
Just keep swimming, swimming, swimming."
—Dory, in *Finding Nemo*

HEY DUDES,

One of the earliest learning opportunities you get in life is figuring out how to navigate through disappointment, adversity, and failure. Among the first challenges you encounter is mastering the skill of walking—literally putting one foot in front of the other. In most cases, it takes a number of unsuccessful attempts that land you on your diapered bottom before you can manage to let go and take one precarious step, which leads to a bunch of wobbly steps in a row, which leads to walking confidently, which leads to racing around like a pro. Without the tools to be resilient, you'd still be sitting on the floor, the whole world passing you by.

When you encounter tough times in your life and find yourself knocked on your behind—and you invariably will—once again you need to find that inner strength to pick yourself up and move forward, putting one foot in front of the other, rather than dwelling on setbacks. The road to success is a bumpy one, and misfortune, rejection, and criticism are all part of normal everyday life. Knowing how to handle adverse situations adeptly is a significant key to success.

We love you all the way to the moon and back, but we also understand that if we protected you from every hurt or failure, you wouldn't be able to develop the skills you will need to be resilient and self-reliant human beings. It's mighty important to be exposed to experiences of loss and change as a child, as that's the only way you will become equipped to get over things and move on. Dad's friend, Dr. Daniel DeWitt, a psychologist at Shields Meneley, an executive consulting firm in Chicago, says, "Experiencing trauma or adversity early in life with appropriate support makes you stronger. In life, it's like a flu shot or inoculation so your body can handle shock more easily when it happens."

We've tried to help you gain perspective from adversity, and move forward with a positive attitude. It's perfectly okay to feel sad or hurt or sorry for yourself for a brief while—you wouldn't be human if you didn't let it out from time to time. But then you need to take responsibility for getting back up and having the courage to take that first wobbly step, as difficult and uncomfortable as it may be.

One reason kids have developed such a sense of entitlement is because parents almost reflexively swoop in to save the day or shelter their children from anything but praise and positive outcomes, regardless of effort or performance. In fact, one of your favorite comics, Jerry Seinfeld, put on a serious face in a recent interview in *Parade*, saying, "We refuse to let our children have problems. Problem-solving is the most important skill to develop for success in life, and we for some reason can't stand it if our kids have a situation that they need to 'fix.' Let them struggle—it's a gift." J.K. Rowling put it even more succinctly with words that came out of Albus Dumbledore's mouth in *Harry Potter and the Goblet of Fire:* "Numbing the pain for a while will make it worse when you finally feel it."

The truth is, not everyone is invited to the party. Everybody isn't a winner all the time. Only one kid can be picked as the lead in the show. You can't always be first. It's a fact of life, and the earlier you accept that, the better prepared you will be to bounce back when things don't go your way.

At the risk of sounding callous and insensitive, we adopted the "Suck it up, dude," philosophy when you were little boys. Of course we're right there by your side if a situation is physically dangerous or your rights have been compromised, but we treat garden variety disappointment or failure by giving you an ear to listen briefly to your ranting and wallowing, a hug, and an honest "Suck it up, dude." We help you assess your strengths, encourage you to believe in your abilities, and then it's up to you to map out a solution and muster the self-confidence to move forward.

We've never been proponents of participation trophies, given to everybody just so no one's feelings get hurt. The year your team won the local AA division Little League championship? You bet you deserved your trophies! Other years? Fun season, valiant effort, superb sportsmanship, but you and your teammates didn't deserve trophies simply for showing up. By awarding one to everyone, the reward becomes diluted and less special for the winners, and everyone else becomes conditioned to expect rewards without success. And you sure don't get rewarded and recognized just for the mere fact that you showed up anywhere else in life!

We've given you the freedom and "permission" to be unsuccessful—so long as you've put forth your best effort. That support and encouragement has helped you take even greater pride in your accomplishments because you know that they are truly your own. Because we don't instantly rush in to rescue you from failure, you have connected the fact that you are accountable for your choices and actions, and you have become empowered to figure out ways to right the ship when it's off course. Looking to place blame elsewhere—on your luck, your timing, your job, your genes, your education, your environment—abdicates responsibility and hinders your ability to move forward productively.

Likewise, complaining and whining is ineffectual, and plays no part in helping you get back on track. What's the line we often borrow from Jimmy Dugan, the manager in *A League of Their Own*? "There's no crying in baseball!"

Adversity and failure are wonderful teachers, often impelling people to greater heights. The first step, however, is to acknowledge and accept reality. Perhaps you failed a test. Maybe you continually can't seem to make ends meet every month. Or you repeatedly get far down the job interview path, but never get offered the job. All these instances are giving you valuable feedback that you are doing something that you need to change or are following a course that you need to modify. Recognizing that you need to do something different is critical because, if you don't make adjustments, you will persistently get the same unsuccessful results. Perhaps you'd do better on the next test if you sat closer to the front of the classroom so you could record more useful notes, or you would benefit by breaking up your studying into shorter chunks. Maybe you need an iPhone application to keep track of your expenditures throughout the month, or it could be time you looked for a less expensive apartment. Or it might be that you need some interview training so that you stop turning off potential employers by treating job interviews like therapy sessions. In any case, you need to admit that something isn't working, and then it's your responsibility to figure out how to make a shift or refinement that will yield a more positive outcome.

Sometimes you won't immediately discover the exact solution, but you'll at least know which roads to avoid. Inventor Thomas Edison was able to view this as an advantage. In a 1921 *American Magazine* interview, he explained, "After we had conducted thousands of experiments on a certain project without solving the problem, one of my associates, after we had conducted the crowning experiment and it had proved a failure, expressed discouragement and disgust over our having failed to find out anything." He added, "I cheerily assured him that we had learned something. For we had learned for a certainty that the thing couldn't be done that way, and that we would have to try some other way."

Successful people fail every day. A baseball player with a respectable batting average won't get a hit 7 out of 10 times he steps up to the plate. But he puts on his helmet and his gloves, grabs his bat, takes his stance, and faces the pitcher every time the batting order comes around. As Babe Ruth used to say, "Every strike brings me closer to the next home run." J.K. Rowling was reportedly turned down for a year by publisher after publisher before her agent called with the good news that her book was going see the light of day. In 2007, *Advertising Age* calculated the Harry Potter brand to be worth in excess of $15 billion. The Beatles were rejected by many record labels, most notably Decca Records, which claimed that guitar groups were on their way out and the band had no future in show business. They, of course, went on to become one of the most critically acclaimed and commercially successful bands in the history of pop music.

We have two powerful profiles to share with you, highlighting exceptional examples of resilience and accountability. The first features Patrick Ciriello, the husband of one of Mom's childhood friends, and how he coped with the grim effects of the Great Recession. His hopeful attitude, pragmatic approach, and realistic perspective adroitly equipped him to weather the unprecedented financial crisis that decimated his industry, and allowed him not only to survive, but to land squarely on his feet. The second piece profiles Mike Nardone, a business acquaintance of Dad's, and how he mustered the ability to function in the immediate aftermath of one of the most profoundly devastating days in our country's history. His anguishing first-person account of the events of September 11th is the backdrop for his unimaginable story of putting one wobbly foot in front of the other—and his personal resilience is a microcosm of how his company, the city of New York, and the nation as a whole had to find the courage and confidence to move forward after sustaining such a tragic blow. What's equally remarkable is the genuine humility and character each of these gentlemen possesses. You will undoubtedly admire their positive fortitude.

Onward and upward,
Mama and Dad

PATRICK CIRIELLO

What's the best advice you've ever gotten?

You never get a second chance to make a first impression.

If you were to receive an award, what would you want it to be for?

Father of the Year.

Who or what inspires you?

My wife and daughters.

What do you see as the greatest challenge for the next generation of Americans?

Learning to be flexible and adaptable in a much more global world.

What three (famous) people, living or dead, would you invite to your fantasy dinner party?

My maternal grandfather
My wife's father
Frank Sinatra

I f Patrick Ciriello had a theme song about his life, there's little doubt it would be Frank Sinatra's top-five classic, "That's Life." Except you'd never find Patrick contemplating a situation where he would roll himself up in a big ball and die. That's just not his style.

Patrick faces adversity head-on. As he explains, "You're going to get punched in the nose at various times in your life, and some punches are going to be harder than others. You've got to have a plan, get back up, dust yourself off, and figure it out, because nobody's going to do it for you."

Patrick's pragmatic philosophy has been an inspiring drumbeat during tough times, most recently in 2008 when he was one of over 150,000 people in the financial services industry who lost not just their jobs, but essentially their careers, as the commercial mortgage-backed securities industry vanished and world financial markets seized up amid the disastrous credit crisis.

Patrick had been climbing his career ladder as a commercial mortgage banker for 12 years when the ax fell. "When I started in 1996, I was originating loans from $1 million to $15 million in value," he says. "By the time I was let go, I was a senior banker at JP Morgan, doing $100 million, $200 million deals with large sophisticated borrowers. For 12 years, it was basically onward and upward. There had been speed bumps along the way, but nothing like what happened in 2008."

The first inkling that something was awry came in the spring of 2007, when Patrick sensed some irregular market behavior. "I was talking to my trader who was telling me that spreads were widening, and when I called down to the desk for pricing on loans, I noticed that they weren't as aggressive," he recalls. "I didn't know what was going on, but I could sense something wasn't right."

The subtle rumblings were unsettling enough to convince Patrick to rethink the purchase of a beach house he and his wife, Marcia, were considering, and instead bank his 2007 bonus. He also began to tighten the belt a bit on expenses. "I am a saver by nature, and so we started hunkering down a little bit more," he mentions. "Nothing super-dramatic like selling the house or cutting drastically, but little things here and there, just in anticipation that maybe things weren't going to be as good as they were."

When January of 2008 rolled around, even though the securitization markets had begun to decline, Patrick received another bonus from JP Morgan. "This was before Bear Stearns. It was still at the point when nobody realized the extent of what was coming," remembers Patrick. "If you think back, every time there had been a hiccup—whether it was 9/11 or the fall of 1998—within a couple of months things had bounced back, and I think the mindset at the company was that by April, May, June, maybe things will start getting back to normal. So they paid us our bonuses." Patrick, ever the prudent saver, banked that extra compensation as well.

But talk about "riding high in April, shot down in May." Within weeks, Patrick found himself seated-belted on a roller coaster ride that ultimately went off the rails and crashed. "I took that bonus in early 2008 as an indication that they were paying the guys who they want to stay around," reasons Patrick. "So I was feeling pretty good, even knowing that things weren't great. Then it went from, 'We're buying Bear Stearns . . . hooray!' to a month later, they do their politics and figure out who's going to run groups. And they put a Bear Stearns guy in charge of the real estate group, which was just a shocker. So when that happened in early May, I realized that the chances of me or anyone at JP Morgan staying were going to be pretty slim."

Almost immediately, Patrick saw the unmistakable writing on the wall and knew his days were numbered. "I had been through a couple of mergers, and it's a lot of politics. Basically, if your guy makes it, you make it," he recounts. "But this one was different, because it was a combination of a market falling apart, a securitization market in just a complete free fall—going from 100 miles an hour to 0 miles an hour—and then you combine that with the merger with an investment bank that has a group that does exactly what you do."

Although he was expecting to be let go, he says that when D-day finally arrived in June, it was still tough. "The night before, they called and said, 'Hey, make sure you're around tomorrow,' which we had all been sort of waiting for and wondering what the hell was taking so long," he shares. "You get the standard speech and the HR guy is there to answer any questions. But it's just a sad day. A depressing day," he admits. "I had been at JP Morgan for nine years. You look around your group and these are people I worked 10, 12 hours a day with for years. You've built up a group and you've been through difficult times, and now everybody's going their own way."

Once it was official, Patrick's first instinct was to spring into action. "I didn't spend a lot of time feeling sorry for myself. Maybe a day. You've got to pick yourself up, dust yourself off, and figure it out."

Despite the fact that he would be receiving severance pay for nine months—plus, by his calculation, his savings would sustain the family in its current lifestyle for about four years—Patrick immediately set out to cut expenses, both large and small. Instantly gone was the nanny who had been helping with the couple's two young daughters while Marcia had been running her portrait and event photography business.

"I looked at all our expenses to figure out what we were spending on everything from school to housing to food, just looking for things we could cut or where we could economize," reports Patrick. "I called my insurance agent and clipped a couple thousand dollars off the insurance bill simply by changing carriers. Marcia and I went on a family plan for the phone, which we should've done years before, and we saved over 100 bucks a month. We even did small things like just cutting back and trying to be a little leaner and meaner."

Marcia sought to shore up the income side of the budget by adding more time to her work schedule, and in the back of his mind, Patrick knew that in the worst case, he could fall back on his savings. "I had saved over those 12 years and built up a pot of money," he reasons. "Not that you ever want to dip into it, but that's what it's there for."

Patrick is no stranger to adversity, and he's quick to admit that powerful lessons learned through two traumatic ordeals earlier in life helped him keep his chin up during his extended unemployment. The first heartbreaking misfortune occurred in the 1980s when Patrick was a senior in high school. A gifted and passionate baseball player, he had been training tirelessly with the goal of becoming a pro, even scoring a tryout with the New York Yankees.

"And then one day before a game, the coach was hitting warm-ups on the infield, and I was playing first base. The ball took a bad hop and cocked me in the eye," laments Patrick. "I didn't think much of it, but my eye puffed up and I had to go to the hospital. Turned out it had messed up my retina to the point where they couldn't repair it, and I have a blind spot in my left eye. The doctor said I wouldn't be able to play competitive sports. So for me as a 17-year-old, that was my world and everything I wanted. And it was gone in a flash."

A much more profound anguish rocked Patrick's world in 2006, however, when his second child was born 16 weeks early, weighing only one and a half pounds. Baby Isabella spent 88 days in the NICU, alternately reaching euphoric milestones and suffering harrowing challenges and setbacks, before she found the path reserved expressly for survivors and champions. Patrick says that living through those 88 days changed his perspective on life forever.

"When I lost my job and things were going really badly, I looked at Isabella and I realized things could have been so much worse," confides Patrick. "She's here and healthy and normal. My kids are healthy and everybody's happy. While the job thing was traumatic, in the scheme of things it seemed to pale by comparison. Quite honestly, that put the whole job thing in perspective."

He continues, "There are going to be times when things certainly don't go my way, or things are going to happen that I don't like. I just think you have to fight through obstacles. You have to take something negative and turn it into a positive or a strength." He goes on, "Some problems are going to be huge, like Isabella, and you don't have control over them and you just have to work through them and figure them out. And then there's things like getting smacked in the eye with a ball and ending your baseball career and then saying, 'Okay, now what? My whole identity is gone.' But it's the same things. It's not the end of the world. Nobody died."

Getting a new job was the next order of business, a challenge that initially seemed promising. "My first inclination was to look in my field, or at least in real estate finance, and see what was out there," says Patrick. "And in July and August, I was getting interviews, getting called back for second interviews. So I felt, 'Okay, this isn't bad.' Plus it was summertime, and I got to see my kids a lot more." In early September, he was called back for a third interview with the real estate finance department at a large homebuilding corporation. "I was thinking, 'It's not going to be the same thing I was doing, it's a little different, but it could be fun or it could be interesting.'"

And then, within days, the opportunity bubble burst. Lehman Brothers collapsed, becoming the largest bankruptcy in the country's history, throwing the financial markets into a reckless tailspin. As Patrick describes, "Then AIG went down. And the week after that it was Wachovia. And then Washington Mutual. And Fannie Mae and Freddie Mac. From mid-September to early or mid-October, basically the whole world changed within those three or four weeks."

When Patrick was finally able to reconnect with the homebuilder about the job he had interviewed for three times, they were brutally honest and told him the company was in survival mode and obviously couldn't justify the idea of hiring. "That's when the lightbulb went on. I realized I had to broaden my horizons, cast a wider net," he recalls. "That meant either potentially relocating, which I didn't want to do, or looking at other industries. During those first four or five months, I thought I was going to be able to stay in the real estate field. But with the whole financial industry blowing up, I realized that might be difficult.

"A lot of people were in the same boat," he acknowledges. "There were thousands of people doing securitization and commercial real estate who suddenly didn't have that specific industry to work in, and they were now trying to move within the real estate industry when things were going south. I could have kept trying and maybe I would have found something, but I looked at it from an analytical perspective and said, 'What are the odds?'"

It was clearly time for Plan B. Patrick's next challenge was to identify his transferrable skills and start looking for work in an industry that might be in better shape. "When you do something for so long, you don't really step back and think about what skills you have or what you're doing," he confesses. "It's like going back to the drawing board and seeing where you can adapt and be flexible and transfer your skill set to another industry."

That's when the career counseling services that JP Morgan had included in the severance package became invaluable. Patrick says having access to the outplacement center was critical over the next few months. "I basically treated it like a job," he recalls. "I was going in four days a week, from 9:30 to 4:30. I was on the computer, calling people, meeting people, trying to move the ball down the field."

The career counselor he was assigned coached him to scope out other industries. "She'd tell me to just keep talking to people, keep meeting with people. You'll discover things," he shares. She encouraged Patrick to research areas that had been of interest to him, and industries that might be hiring, and she suggested that he list his skills to see which might be transferrable. "She started me on the process," says a grateful Patrick. "She was so busy that I couldn't see her every day, so I had to take the bull by the horns and do a lot of it myself. But I would check in with her from time to time."

Autumn turned to winter without any promise of employment, though, and 2009 began with Patrick still out of work. "You're beating your head against the wall every day. Going in, calling people, trying to network," notes Patrick. "I think it's hard enough trying to find a job in general when you get laid off. I mean, for most people it's traumatic. But to get laid off—and then a month or two into it have the worst financial crisis since the Great Depression in combination—just makes it doubly or triply challenging."

Patrick credits his wife with comforting him on his down days. "Marcia was incredibly supportive," he remembers. "She would say, 'Look, it's not you, it's the economy. This is unprecedented. Just keep plugging along. You can't take it personally.' And I wasn't. I realized what was going on."

Much as Patrick resisted feeling sorry for himself, it was hard to stay positive as January came and went with nothing hopeful on the horizon. He was mindful that his severance pay was about to run out, and that wasn't the only bad news. It looked like the bottom was going to fall out of the stock market yet again, and Patrick's savings had decreased in value by some 40 percent since the previous summer. And with the market in freefall once more, companies were decidedly not stepping up to the plate to bring on new hires.

"I could be the greatest thing since sliced bread, but who's got the nerve to stick their neck out there and hire people?" recognizes Patrick. "So now it's February and I'm wondering how much longer this is going to go on. Another six months? Another nine months? You knew at some point it was going to bottom, you just didn't know how long it was going to take."

For a thankful, relieved Patrick, the answer was not much longer. His tenacious networking had led him to a series of interviews for a financial advisor position at AllianceBernstein, a global investment management firm in New York. Although it would be a brand-new job for Patrick, his career counselor viewed going to work for a large, well-known, public company as a prudent move.

"She saw names like Nomura Securities and JP Morgan on my résumé," recalls Patrick. "And she said that AllianceBernstein would maintain the integrity of my résumé. One of my concerns was, 'What happens if commercial real estate comes back? Is leaving real estate to do something different going to hurt me?' And her answer was, 'Not at all. Nobody's going to fault you for going to work at one of the biggest money managers in the country.'"

Patrick was offered the position in March and started working at Bernstein in April—10 months after he had been let go from

JP Morgan. Not only is the job different—he is now responsible for gathering new assets—but his total compensation is less than it had been. "Now there's no bonus unless I sign people up and they bring their assets over," he explains. "So it's going to be a process of building that up and getting clients, and that's going to take a while."

Still, Patrick considers himself lucky. "Knowing how bad things were, and looking at some of my friends who are still out of work or who aren't making money, I feel incredibly grateful that Bernstein hired me at the depths of the market and decided to go forward," he reflects. "I'm happy to be here and it's a great company. I'm learning something new. I'm developing a new skill set." He adds, "We'll see where things are in two years, but for now, it's better to have a job than not have a job. It's good to be working."

Many of his former colleagues haven't been as fortunate. "I know guys who are out of work going on two years, and they're still saying, 'I'm focusing on real estate. I'm trying to find something in the industry.' I don't know if the thought has even crossed their minds about switching industries," reports Patrick. "Some have found jobs here and there, a lot less pay than what they were making before, working at much smaller places. Some are still unemployed. Some are trying to do consulting on their own. It's interesting to see the different courses people have taken."

True to character, Patrick found an upside to his extended job search. "The silver lining in all of it was being able to reconnect with my kids and just seeing what goes on day to day. I wasn't traveling. I was home for dinner every night. I took them to school. When would I ever have nine months to spend with my five-year-old and my three-year-old, basically uninterrupted?" he asks.

What other perspective would you expect from a guy who undeniably knows how to pick himself up and get back in the race?

MIKE NARDONE

What's the best advice you've ever gotten?

You get out of life what you put into it.

If you were to receive an award, what would you want it to be for?

For being a mentor.

Who or what inspires you?

People who are not given the same tools as everyone else, whether it's a handicap, a diversity, an injury.

What do you see as the greatest challenge for the next generation of Americans?

Failure to put in the work and just expecting the same results—or greater.

What three (famous) people, living or dead, would you invite to your fantasy dinner party?

Sir Edmund Hillary
Mel Brooks
Abraham Lincoln

Like almost everyone who awakened in the Northeast on September 11th, 2001, Mike Nardone vividly remembers the picture-perfect weather on that Tuesday morning. "Stunningly beautiful," he describes. He had taken the train into Manhattan from his Connecticut home, and emerging from the Fulton Street subway station, he was dazzled by the bright sunshine and striking blue sky. He walked through the promenade at the World Trade Center to get to his office in the human resources department at American Express, across the street in the World Financial Center.

"I remember so well looking around and seeing everybody out having coffee," recounts Mike, who had only recently joined Amex as vice president of HR for the small business and consumer travel segments and the risk management portfolio. "I was really happy that day because I had only been with the company a couple of months, but I felt like things were coming along. I had come out of a meeting on Monday that had gone really well, and I actually remember specifically being really happy, just going to work."

Mike, in his early 40s at the time, headed up to his desk on the 47th floor a few minutes after 8:00, greeted his boss and began typing an e-mail to a friend in the U.K., telling him how much he liked his new job and company.

"I'm at the keyboard typing, and then I heard this most incredible thud I've ever heard in my life," recalls Mike. "Not an explosion, but like a deadened thud. The whole office shook, and I thought, 'What the hell was that?' My credenza was against the wall, and the books came off." Mike abandoned the e-mail and stepped out of his office at the same moment his boss came flying out into the hallway, eyes wide and panic-stricken.

"My boss had been on the phone talking to a guy that he was going to offer a presidency to. They were literally coordinating an offer," shares Mike. "And he comes flying out and he says, 'Get out of the building!'" Mike's boss's office faced the World Trade Center, and Mike looked toward his window to see what had spooked his boss. "I could see smoke and paper coming out of the World Trade Center," remembers Mike. "And I thought, 'What the hell just happened?' and without my asking, my boss just said, 'A plane.'"

Mike's initial assumption was that a small plane had accidentally struck the tower. Following his boss's instruction, he got on the elevator, which stopped a few floors below. Says Mike, "Another guy got on, and he said, 'I saw it. It was a plane.'" Mike asked if it was a small plane, and the guy shook his head. "He said, 'No, it was a big plane.' I didn't believe him," Mike discloses. "I thought he was crazy."

When he got out of the building, Mike ran into Al Kelly, the president of American Express, who said he thought a plane had accidentally hit the World Trade Center.

"I remember distinctly looking up and seeing all the smoke. I didn't see any flames, just smoke piling all over the place," recalls Mike. "I thought, 'Where did the plane go?' because I figured it had to have gone through the building." Mike looked over toward Wall Street, horrified that the plane must have crashed in that area. "Never in my wildest dreams did I think the plane would disintegrate in the building," he admits.

A stunned crowd gathered and looked up toward the top of the damaged building, which was quickly becoming engulfed in billowing black smoke. Flames would leap out of the building from time to time. Everyone assumed it had been an isolated tragic accident.

"I'll never forget what transpired next," confides Mike. "I'm looking up, and then out of the right corner of my eye, I see another plane, and it's banking at an unnatural angle. I saw it come down the Hudson River, and then it banked in front of this building, so I couldn't see it. And then all I saw was the biggest explosion I've ever seen in my life in this building. It had come through and exploded out this way down where we were. I knew instantly that it was a terrorist attack. At that exact moment," reveals Mike.

The crowd scattered like ants, and sheer pandemonium befell the area. People scrambled desperately for their own safety, trampling others in their way. Mike's instinct was to escape the island, and he ran toward the ferry near the World Financial Center. "The ferry was swamped with people to the point where it was going to sink," reports Mike. "The ferry pilot basically said, 'We're going, we're going, we're going,' and when he gunned the engine, there were people hanging on the side of the boat because they were literally jumping onto the ferry." One executive from Amex had to be pulled back to land by a colleague, as she had only one leg over the railing when the ferry took off, in a determined attempt to flee.

People were running and screaming. "I don't think there was a person on the ground who didn't think we were under attack," says Mike. "And I didn't know where to go, because I was brand new to the company. I wasn't even sure which way north was, for a second. All I knew was subway, walkway, office."

Mike ran around the corner and looked up. "What I remember distinctly was that one of the buildings the plane had hit square between the floors, and I thought the building was secure," he shares. "But the other plane hit in the corner, and I thought that building was going to topple over; it wasn't going to hold."

He had no clue where to go. "Because I had left the building in a hurry, I had no wallet. No cell phone. No keys. No money. Nothing," he describes. "And I just said, 'Well, I guess I should walk.'"

He headed to a nearby park and remembers sitting on a bench, feeling intensely overwhelmed. "I was thinking, 'I'm in human resources. Our building is still standing. I must have some responsibility to this company and people. I should probably stay here and see what I'm supposed to do,'" he confesses. "Because I thought that's what my job was."

What happened next will stay with Mike for the rest of his life. "I'm sitting on this bench watching, and I thought I saw debris coming out of the building. I was hoping that it was debris. But in my heart I knew it wasn't," discloses Mike. "It was people. People jumping out. It was ones and twos. And then I saw what has stayed with me and I'll never forget. People holding hands. Twos. Fours. Threes. And they were all dying." His voice breaks.

Mike remembers a woman standing near him in the park, collapsing to the ground, screaming, "Why are they doing it?" Mike went over, put his arms around her, and buried her head in his chest to shield her view of what he was witnessing. "I remember watching, and thinking, 'These people are dying, and somebody has to watch them die.' I watched every single one come out. I just felt like I owed it to them." He continues, "I would want somebody to remember this if I had to do that kind of thing. Imagine the choice these people are making. It was just awful. I don't know how many people jumped, but it was enough that you'd never forget it in your life. Thank God I didn't have to see any hit the ground, because they would just disappear when they got to the 20th floor, disappear amongst the shorter buildings."

The next thing Mike remembers was seeing something crack atop the South Tower, and he was sure the whole building was about to topple over. Except it didn't. Almost instantaneously, the top floors began to collapse into one another. "I didn't expect it to pancake in on each other," explains Mike. "Once it started, it just went straight in on itself. And then I knew what was coming next. The biggest explosion in the world. And all I did was run."

Mike ran northward as fast as his feet would take him, trying to outrun the cloud of smoke, dust, and debris. Lucky to be at the front end of it, he ran and ran and ran. He found the running path on the West Side along the Hudson River, and joined hundred of others running in a furious fight for their lives. He remembers a generous street vendor handing out water bottles from his cart to people running by so they could wash their eyes or their faces. Mike grabbed a bottle and thanked the man as he cleaned the dust from his face. He was out of breath and his heart was pounding. He went a bit further and then stopped to collect himself, still having no idea where he was heading. As he turned his gaze back toward the destruction, he saw the top of the second tower crack, and watched as that building then collapsed on itself.

"Then I thought, 'Well, this is the worst day ever. We have to regroup as a country,'" recalls Mike. "At that time I thought tens of thousands of people had been killed." Mike just kept hustling north toward Grand Central Station. As he got further from the devastation, he saw opportunistic street vendors charging $10 a bottle for water. He tried to duck into a hotel to wash up and use the restroom, but the security force had blocked all the doors to everyone except guests holding room keys. "You couldn't go anywhere, and obviously you couldn't take the subway, so I was just walking and walking," he reports.

As he made his way toward Grand Central, he could see throngs of people running toward him down Park Avenue. "I thought I was going to be crushed," he remembers. "I ran and hid in the alcove of a building, and I was screaming, 'What's wrong? Why are you running?'" Someone told him that there had been a bomb threat at Grand Central. Eventually, the area was cleared, and the station reopened. "There was only one train going north," recounts Mike, who hopped aboard. "It packed with as many people as it could. And then a woman just yelled, 'Let's go, let's go, let's go! We've got no more space!' and the thing took off."

For the next hour and 50 minutes, as the train made its stops through New York and suburban Connecticut, there was not so much as a peep on board. "I've never experienced anything like that," says Mike. "Every single person just sat, staring straight ahead. There was no ticket person that showed up. Nothing. Just silence."

When he got off at his stop, Mike saw armed guards with machine guns at the train station. Without car keys, a cell phone, or a wallet, he managed to use a pay phone to call his wife, who had been released from work when the news hit. She was aware he worked in the World Financial Center as opposed to the World Trade Center, but she didn't know his fate until she got his call. Their reunion at the train station was emotional. "I think that's the first time I let my guard down, but even then I still couldn't believe what was happening," shares Mike. "I was having a hard time processing the whole day. But you realize you're okay, and you just appreciate everything."

Mike's dad confused the names of the buildings, and had instantly assumed the worst. "My father was in church praying," Mike notes. "I called him as soon as I got home, and my dad nearly fainted on the phone. He could not believe that I was calling him. My brothers were the same. They all thought that that was it, I was dead."

The phone kept ringing, with friends literally shocked and relieved when Mike would answer. Shortly, though, Mike didn't want to talk about it anymore. He felt the need to go to the gym and run. But he found no peace at the gym, where he remembers everybody asking questions out of morbid curiosity. Sickened, he walked out and went home.

And that was the moment Mike Nardone took life by the reins and snapped into action. "When that sort of stuff happens, people either respond or they don't," reflects Mike. "So I immediately started working the phones. I started reconnecting with my colleagues." Mike relied on skills he had developed in his previous job at an Internet company. "I knew what it was like not to have an office. I knew what it was like to make things happen by yourself, without needing a formal work space."

He put together a call tree and started reaching out to colleagues. "I knew what my job was," he asserts. "I knew that I had a set of responsibilities. I could've just not done anything. I could've just sat there and waited for somebody to call me, but I was literally working the phone that afternoon and the next day, trying to figure out where the team was."

Being the new guy gave Mike a bit of motivation to get to work. "You know, new to the company, I figured if I didn't do something, I'd probably get fired. So maybe there was a fear factor," he admits. "But I mean, I've been that way my whole life. Just keep it simple, don't try to be a hero, just focus on what's in front of you and what you can control. And at that time, what I could control was calling people and trying to build call trees and trying to connect with the leaders."

The group immediately set up two conference calls a day, at noon and at 5:00 P.M. For the first two days, the objective was simply to locate team members and make sure everyone was okay.

"I don't think I did anything special," notes Mike. "I was just focused on what I knew had to get done, because I didn't know what else to do. I just felt like that's what you're supposed to do. You're supposed to get organized, get on with what you've got to do."

Mike is quick to point out that diving back into work wasn't an avoidance strategy to block out the tremendous emotional impact of the trauma. "In fact, I wrote a journal," he shares. "I drew pictures. My father told me to do that. He said to write down what I remembered. And I did. I don't look at it a lot, but every once in a while I do."

Out of roughly 3,800 American Express employees who had worked at the World Financial Center, 11 lost their lives on 9/11. According to Mike, the shell of the building was left mostly undamaged, except for several hundred windows that had blown out. The major structural damage was internal, caused by a girder that had flown off the World Trade Center and pierced the building across the street like a torpedo, impaling a number of floors that had to be rebuilt.

Mike's group was without formal workspace for a couple of weeks before the company secured makeshift offices in several locations. Mike wound up commuting to an office in Parsippany, New Jersey. "I look back at that time," he reflects, "and I have to say that the company was incredibly organized and incredibly focused on people, and it didn't really care that much whether it made money in those first two or three months." He adds, "It was more about, 'Can we get our employees reconnected? Can we help them? Can we understand what the commuting issues are?' I felt blessed that I worked for that company. It has a culture. It believes in people. It has its priorities right."

Mike shared that priority. "What I did after 9/11 was listen to my colleagues," he recounts. "I have three very good colleagues who have told me many times the reason that they got through 9/11 was because I made their days enjoyable by listening, and encouraging them, and trying to make some humor sometimes."

He continues, "I think I've always done that. I listen, and I try to mentor or help where I can."

After a month or so, Amex leased offices for Mike's group at 40 Wall Street, and Mike went into Manhattan to check out the space. "A month after 9/11, it was still a war zone down there, still smoldering," he confirms. A colleague convinced Mike to go up to the highest point in the building, and somehow the two managed to go all the way up to the tiny glass-enclosed spire, more than 70 stories above lower Manhattan. "We looked down. And that was the first time I saw the totality of what had happened," recalls Mike. "I saw, from an aerial view, what had happened. It wasn't just the Twin Towers that were gone; the amount of destruction in the surrounding areas was unbelievable. I hadn't quite realized it until I looked at the space. We just stared."

About a year after the attack, Mike received a promotion, largely based on his caring responsiveness during the company's darkest days. "Sometimes it's how people respond that creates opportunities. I know I earned the promotion, but I also know that it was opportunistic and I still feel a little bit weird about that." He adds, "I ended up being seen as somebody who was resilient, who just focused on what had to get done. My boss told me that it was my ability to just focus and block out what I had to block out and just do what I needed to do. He was impressed by that, and I know for a fact that it leap-frogged me above other people."

American Express ultimately welcomed its employees back to the repaired World Financial Center almost 15 months after the tragic events unfolded. The 11 employees who had lost their lives that day were remembered in a beautiful service, and an 11-sided granite memorial entitled "Eleven Tears" was unveiled in the lobby.

The way Mike handled 9/11 is the way he has always handled life. "Listen, I don't have the biggest IQ in the world. But what I do have is the ability to just keep pushing forward, no matter what. I learned that from my dad. He taught me that whatever you do, just do the best that you can, and know that you have to put in the energy and the time to do it."

His wife puts it best. She simply calls Mike "The Little Engine That Could."

— 7 —

SELF-DISCIPLINE & PATIENCE

"Isn't delayed gratification the definition of maturity?"
—Carrie Bradshaw, in *Sex and the City*

Hi Guys,

Can you think of a more overindulged, undisciplined terror than one Miss Veruca Salt in the 1971 film, *Willy Wonka and the Chocolate Factory*, who, upon being deemed a bad egg by the Eggdicator in Wonka's Golden Egg Room, was swiftly sent plummeting down the garbage chute into the furnace? Among the acquisitions she imperiously demanded her father procure were a golden ticket, a golden goose, an Oompa Loompa, pink macaroons, a million balloons, performing baboons, presents, prizes of all shapes and sizes, not to mention the whole world. While her entitled attitude and covetous wish list are assuredly objectionable, what's more heinous are the time frame and means she demands. "Don't care how," she repeatedly blusters, "I want it NOW!"

Unfortunately, this attitude—even in a tempered, less obnoxious form—is one of the root causes of the debt epidemic that plagues so many Americans. We live in a culture of materialism and immediacy, and we've somehow lost our collective ability to delay gratification. The pervasive mindset is to charge or finance whatever your heart desires, and worry about how to pay for it later. It's a dangerous impulse with potentially devastating, long-term financial repercussions.

Being able to delay gratification is a learned skill. It requires the ability to think before you act, to understand the potential consequences of your actions, and most importantly, to have patience. In a famous research study conducted in the late 1960s called "The Marshmallow Test," psychologist Dr. Walter Mischel, offered a tempting choice to four-year-olds at a preschool on the Stanford University campus. He told them they could have one marshmallow now, or if they were willing to wait for several minutes while he stepped out of the room, they could have two when he returned. Predictably, some kids instantly grabbed the marshmallow and ate it. Other more patient kids waited for the additional reward, some employing distractive measures like covering their eyes, playing under the table or singing *Sesame Street* songs to pass the time. When Dr. Mischel and his researchers followed up on the children when they were graduating from high school, he found the kids who had been able to wait for the extra marshmallow to be better able to cope with the pressures of life; they were more self-assertive, socially competent, and academically successful. In fact, the children who had been able to wait for the extra marshmallow had S.A.T. scores that were, on average, 210 points higher than scores for the grabbers.

At its core, self-discipline is the ability to put off one gratification for the chance to get a different gratification at a later time. Without restraint and self-control, your needs and desires can easily exceed your resources, putting at risk things like your home, your car, your credit rating, and your ability to save for retirement.

Developing the discipline to delay gratification is critical to financial self-sufficiency, and the only tried-and-true way to do this is to control spending by creating and faithfully adhering to a personal or household budget. In its simplest terms, a budget is a sustainable financial plan that balances income and spending. The first step in creating a budget is to realistically calculate your net income, which means figuring out your take-home pay, after all taxes and deductions have been subtracted. You no doubt remember the shocking horror of your first official payroll check, when you realized that a significant chunk had been allocated to entities other than you! Income might also be in the form of a bonus, a gift, an inheritance, a tax refund, or the proceeds of the sale of an asset—as long as you actually have the cash in hand or in your bank account. Don't make the mistake of optimistically counting an expected bonus or the amount of an anticipated sale as budgetary income!

The next step is to allocate funds for your housing expenses, whether it's a rent payment or the total cost of your mortgage plus property taxes. A reasonable rule of thumb is to spend no more than 30 percent of your net income on housing.

Your next priority is to allocate another 30 percent of your net income to savings, dividing the money evenly among three distinct accounts.

- The first account is for *long-term savings*—a nest egg—to be used for special significant expenditures, such as a down payment on a home, a new car, or future college tuition costs.
- The second account is for *short-term savings*, which is essentially a cushion to cover irregular expenses like vacations, gifts, and home improvement costs; and unanticipated expenses like home or auto repairs.
- The third account is for *retirement savings* like a 401k or IRA, in which the money grows over a long period without your having to pay taxes until you withdraw the funds. By law, you cannot withdraw the money in a retirement account until you are age 59½, or you will pay a 10 percent penalty.

It's often helpful to have these savings allocations deposited directly from your paycheck into specific bank accounts so you are not tempted to spend the funds. Out of sight, out of mind.

Retirement may seem so far off that you think there's no need for you to stash away money today that you could instead be spending on more exciting or immediately useful expenses. But it's absolutely critical to have the discipline to begin investing for retirement from a young age, and here's why. Let's say you started saving for retirement at age 15 by depositing $100 into some type of retirement account, and you increased your contribution each year by $100 for the next 49 years (so you'd be depositing $200 at age 16, $300 at age 17, all the way up to $5,000 at age 64). When you turned 65, assuming a 10 percent average compounded annual rate of return, you would have $1,353,329 in the account, from contributions totaling $127,500. Now let's run a similar illustration, starting instead from age 30, with an initial deposit of $100, and annual contributions continually increasing by $100. Under that scenario, again assuming a 10 percent average compounded annual return, you would have $289,439 in your retirement account at age 65, having invested $63,000 over 35 years. By delaying for 15 years your commitment to saving, and missing out on the powerful benefit of compound interest over that time, you would have lost out on over $1 million.

In addition to investing for retirement from a young age, history shows that it's equally critical to exercise patience during volatile markets and keep your retirement funds continually invested to benefit from compounding. Unnerving and frustrating as it sometimes may be, focus on your long-term objectives rather than reacting impulsively or emotionally to short-term events or market fluctuations. If you try to time the market by jumping in and out, you run the risk of missing out on some of the best performing days, which can have a dramatic impact on your return. According to a 2009 report by Ned Davis Research, if you had invested $1,000 at the end of September of 1984 in S&P 500 stocks, 25 years later your investment would be worth $11,523, which is a 10.3 percent compounded rate of return. Had you missed the top 25 days in the market during that 25-year period, your initial investment would only be worth $2,750, or a 4.1 percent compounded return.

Getting back to the personal budget, the remaining 40 percent of your net income is what you have left over for all the rest of your expenses. That includes food and clothing; insurance; transportation costs including car payments, gas, parking, or commuting expenses; utility costs like cell phone, cable, Internet, electricity, and heat; charitable donations; personal care products and services; entertainment expenses; as well as the cost of hobbies, lessons, memberships, subscriptions, and miscellaneous incidentals. The key to managing these expenses is having the ability to plan thoughtfully and resist the temptation to indulge in instant gratification. It sometimes means having to say no to certain things, or sacrificing somewhere else in order to keep your budget balanced. You need to weigh your choices and develop an inner voice that gives you the ability to control your impulses and make prudent decisions.

Contrary to both popular belief and what credit card companies would like to have you think, a credit card is not a means to allow you to spend more money than you have. We treat credit cards as "charge cards," meaning we pay off the full balance every month, rather than paying only a portion and leaving the rest as a debt to pay at a future date. For us, credit cards are useful so we don't have to carry substantial cash, and they also help us track expenses throughout the year, which is handy when we are preparing our annual tax return. Unpaid credit card balances are loans that often carry exorbitant annual interest rates, sometimes upward of 15 percent—which is how credit card companies make their money. When you pay with cash, you flip through the paper bills in your wallet and actually feel the money leaving you. Handing over a plastic credit card, on the other hand, registers nothing emotionally, and leaves the door wide open to overspending. It therefore takes discipline to possess a credit card and exercise the restraint to use it solely as a substitute for cash, and not as a means of financing impulse purchases. A safer option is a debit card, which is another alternative payment method to cash. A debit card is linked to your bank account, and funds are withdrawn directly from your balance whenever you use the card. If there's not enough money in the account to cover the expense, the purchase is declined. The bad news is that you can't complete the transaction, but the great news is that you haven't busted your budget or incurred debt.

The profiles for this chapter highlight two couples and how they approach saving, spending, earning, and budgeting. Amy and Howie Blustein are lifelong family friends who consistently use thoughtful prudence and restraint to decide how their two incomes should be allocated to support their family of four. The second couple, Mary and Alberto Lobo, has had a long business relationship with Dad. They emigrated from Portugal more than 50 years ago, and with a strictly disciplined sense of thrift and savings, they have managed to create a financial legacy for the benefit of their children, their grandchildren, and generations beyond. It proves that a combination of hard work, patience, and restraint can truly bring you far down the road to wealth.

Cheerio,
Mama and Dad

AMY BLUSTEIN

What's the best advice you've ever gotten?

If not now, when?

If you were to receive an award, what would you want it to be for?

Having the appropriate work-life balance.

Who or what inspires you?

My kids, my two grandmothers, and Howie.

What do you see as the greatest challenge for the next generation of Americans?

How to live a grounded life while being surrounded by all the crazy technology they have.

What three (famous) people, living or dead, would you invite to your fantasy dinner party?

Bill Clinton
Oprah Winfrey
James Michener

HOWIE BLUSTEIN

What's the best advice you've ever gotten?

If you don't have it, don't spend it.

If you were to receive an award, what would you want it to be for?

Mensch of the Year.

Who or what inspires you?

My kids and my wife.

What do you see as the greatest challenge for the next generation of Americans?

Being respectful with all the technology they have and not losing one-on-one interaction.

What three (famous) people, living or dead, would you invite to your fantasy dinner party?

Albert Einstein
Robin Williams
Frank Sinatra

PRUDENT SAVERS, THOUGHTFUL SPENDERS

A my and Howie Blustein are a credit card company's worst nightmare.

"We charge just about everything–groceries, gas, dinners out, everything," reports Amy, public relations manager at Women & Infants Hospital in Providence, Rhode Island. "And then, at the end of the month, we pay the bill. We pay the whole thing."

Amy and her husband, Howie, a sales manager at Airgas, the largest U.S. distributor of industrial, medical, and specialty gases, have found that credit card companies are more than happy to have them take their business elsewhere. "Every so often we'll be late with the payment, and we'll get a late charge," chuckles Amy. "And I'll call them and go, 'Give me a break, I've never been late before.' And they go, 'Well, sorry.' And I'll say,' You know what, then, we're going to pull our business.' And they're pretty much on the phone going, 'Well, good, because we don't make any money off of you. This is the one month out of six years we've made any money off you.'"

Ever since they married in 1996, maintaining as little debt as possible has been the overarching philosophy for the Blusteins. And for Howie, being debt-free has been the name of the game since childhood, when he heard his father's mantra over and over again: "Don't spend what you don't have."

Amy recalls learning the same valuable lesson from her grandfather, back in her college days. Her parents had gotten her a credit card with an initial $500 limit for her to use in case of an emergency, since she was living four hours from home. "It was my responsibility and I took it very seriously," she remembers. "I rarely used it. And when I did use it, I would pay it off. And every year, the credit card company would increase my credit line, presumably with the hopes that I would start to spend more."

Her junior or senior year, a friend mentioned that she was doing herself a disservice by paying the balance off every month, urging that she carry some debt so future creditors could see that she was responsibly paying it down. Taking the advice to heart, Amy went on a shopping spree, building up a $2,000 balance on the card, which she immediately started paying down. "I was talking to my grandparents and for some reason I mentioned it in front of my grandfather," Amy admits. "I think this might have been the only time he got truly mad at me. He was flippin' angry—couldn't believe I would do such a thing. He wrote me a check, made me pay it off, and then I proceeded to pay him off over the next couple of months. And I've never carried a credit card balance since."

The only debt the couple maintains is the mortgage on their home and a loan on one of their two automobiles, which Howie is adamant about owning rather than leasing. They have recently finished paying off the loan on the other car, yet instead of spending all the extra funds that used to be allocated for car payments, they stash half the amount in an account to be used toward the purchase of a new car someday. "It may sit there for a couple of years," Howie explains, "but it will be there as a cushion in case something else happens in the meantime."

The Blusteins don't view an increase in income as an excuse for an increase in spending; rather they religiously use extra money for paying down debt or put it toward savings. When either gets a raise in salary, for instance, the difference of the raise is directly deposited into one of several savings accounts the couple earmarks for expenses like their son's upcoming bar mitzvah, a family vacation, or education funds for their two children. "Both of our salaries have gone up significantly in the past 10 years, but our lifestyle hasn't changed significantly," insists Amy.

She adds, "Some people are very disciplined and if they get a $1,000 paycheck, they say, 'A hundred dollars goes here and $100 goes to that savings account, $100 goes here, and now I have $700 to spend.' We don't do that. If we have $1,000 coming in, then we have three different direct deposits going into this account, this account, and this account. Because, honestly, if it was in our checking account, which is what we live out of, we would spend it."

For example, Amy says that the most recent holiday bonus she received went into the bar mitzvah fund, with the event less than a year away. "We've been saving for probably five years, knowing full well that we don't want to be carrying debt to pay for our son's bar mitzvah, and knowing full well that three years later we'll be doing it again for our daughter."

The Blusteins live what they deem to be a modest lifestyle by choice. "We could do more than we do, but to us it's very important that we have money to pay for upcoming expenses," explains Amy. "To us, savings is really important."

Setting spending priorities has always been a key to the Blusteins's financial philosophy. "There's a big difference between wants and needs," notes Howie. "Most people are living in the moment."

"We're also a debt society," adds Amy. "People get into trouble when they don't realize that spending, saving, budgeting, and debt are as interconnected as they are."

The couple now keeps a mental accounting of expenses, but for a period a few years ago, they kept a "refrigerator budget," where they posted a piece of paper on the fridge, divided it into columns for food, gas, entertainment, and miscellaneous expenses, and wrote down literally every dime they spent for several months. "When you write everything down like that, you become far more disciplined," insists Amy. "You're less likely to spend the $2 on a Starbucks coffee, as opposed to making it at home."

The exercise confirmed their suspicion that they did not have particularly frivolous spending habits, and now that they are satisfied knowing that, they are comfortable keeping track less formally. "It stays in the back of your head," says Howie. "You say to yourself, 'You know, we've already been out to dinner three times in the past week and a half, so for the rest of the month, we're not going out for dinner.'"

The Blusteins have talked frankly with their kids since they were young about their financial philosophy, teaching them about the discipline of saving, the lesson of not spending what they don't have, and the importance of giving back to the community and people who don't have as much.

"The kids'll say, 'Can we go out for dinner? Can we go do this? Can we go do that?'" reports Amy. "And we'll say, 'You know what, guys? We've already been out to dinner three times this week, so no we can't. Let's stay home.' So it's a check and balance for them also, and they realize that although money seems to grow on a tree, it really doesn't. Communication is vital."

Part of their children's weekly allowance is earmarked for a charitable cause, and for a long time, allowance was given out in quarters, which the kids put directly into giant piggy banks, as almost a forced savings. Amy estimates that each child now has several hundred dollars worth of quarters saved.

The Blusteins try to keep future expenses in mind when considering a splurge. "Sometimes you just have to go, 'Damn it, I just feel like going out and doing it.' But we also realize that, say, in April we're going to Washington, DC and I don't want to have to exercise restraint while we're there. So if that means I have to be careful between now and then, okay."

She says that the kids are also saving their dollars to be able to treat themselves to a special splurge on the family trip to Washington. "The kids happen to have a fair amount of money sitting in their wallets right now in anticipation of our trip."

When it comes to significant expenditures, Howie typically does a lot of homework to make sure they spend wisely. That's why they didn't take the plunge on the new family computer until Apple was offering a special 12-month no-interest deal.

"We waited until we could do it at a period where there was no penalty for charging it out over a year," notes Amy. "It's a big expense. We didn't want to bite the bullet and spend $2,000 in one shot. But we could spend $2,000 over a year."

"That way, it just became part of our monthly budget," adds Howie. "So for the next year, we have an extra $120 that's broken up over the months."

It was Amy who did some unusual homework when the couple were looking to buy their first home shortly after they were married. They discovered that most families in the neighborhood where they wanted to live sent their children to private schools, and even though they had no children at that time, Amy and Howie knew that they would need to consider the future expense of private school if they settled in that particular neighborhood.

"When we were looking to buy that house, I started to call around to some of the private schools to see what their tuition was," Amy shares. "They must have thought I was a crack job! They asked how old our kids were, and I said, 'We don't have any kids. I'm asking because we're looking to buy a home on the East Side, and we know full well that if we do that, we're going to end up sending our kids to private school. So we need to see how that will fit into our budget to determine how much money we can actually spend on a house.' Because if we were looking at $15,000 to $20,000 in tuition, we needed to know that before we purchased the house."

Taking that into consideration, the couple did buy a small home, and the mortgage wound up being less than the rent they had been paying on their apartment. They lived there for three years, eventually needing a larger home to accommodate their growing family. The couple decided to relocate to an area with good public schools, and took pains to calculate a reasonable housing budget.

"There are people who go and meet with a bank or a mortgage broker, and they say, 'Okay, this is our salary,' and they do some quick calculation and say, 'Okay, you could afford a $450,000 home—that's how much you could afford to spend.' And people skip out of there and say, 'Great, I can go spend $450,000 on a house!'" scoffs Amy. "And what the mortgage guy doesn't tell them is, 'That's assuming you don't want to eat and that you have absolutely no other expenses.'"

Amy insists that's not an appealing strategy to them. "We said, 'We will never be house poor.' And we've never been house poor. And we will never be house poor. Ever."

In 2000, the Blusteins bought the 1956 split level where they currently live, and they initially considered not moving in until they added a master bathroom. But nagging prudence kicked in, and they set up a savings account for the eventual home improvement project. Seven years later, they decided it was finally time to do the addition. "I look back on the decision, and think that if we had done the master bathroom when we moved in, we would have ended up with a very, very different layout," reflects Amy about the addition that she loves.

Once the Blusteins decided to do the project, they proceeded judiciously, shopping for an architect and contractor who would work within their established budget. They made careful choices about the materials, using their own discretion about where to be extravagant and where to exercise more restraint. Amy remembers that the project coincided with Howie's 40th birthday, and says that when close family members asked what he might like for a gift, Amy suggested that he would truly appreciate money toward the steam shower he was dreaming of. "It comes down to making the priority," insists Amy. "Were there other things he would have loved to have gotten for his 40th birthday? Absolutely! Absolutely! But this was something he really wanted. And, in order to do that, we needed to sacrifice something else. It was totally worth it."

Are there any plans for further home improvements? Amy fantasizes that if she won $100,000 in the lottery, she'd use the money to upgrade the kitchen for Howie, a talented and appreciated home chef. Ever pragmatic, however, Howie disagrees, saying that a fancy new kitchen would foolishly overvalue the house for the neighborhood, and he'd rather take a modest trip and then put the rest into savings.

Amy admits, "You know, if we really, really wanted to, we could just go out and do the kitchen right now—take out a $75,000 home equity loan and do the kitchen. But right now it's more important for us to know that we can pay for the bar mitzvah comfortably and start the kids off to college comfortably."

Choices. When it comes to spending, saving, budgeting, and debt, it's all about choices.

MARY & ALBERTO LOBO

What's the best advice you've ever gotten?

Make your money work for you.

If you were to receive an award, what would you want it to be for?

Being good parents.

Who or what inspires you?

Our grandchildren.

What do you see as the greatest challenge for the next generation of Americans?

Getting good jobs and being able to save.

What three (famous) people, living or dead, would you invite to your fantasy dinner party?

Our parents
Each other

EPITOME OF THE AMERICAN DREAM

Mary and Alberto Lobo came to the United States for what they saw as abounding opportunity for themselves and future generations. Arriving from Portugal penniless, never in their wildest dreams did they imagine that 50 years of hard work and conscientious saving would enable them to establish a multi-million dollar legacy for their children and grandchildren.

Mary's mother had been born in the United States in 1920, but before her first birthday her family returned to Portugal, where she grew up and eventually married. Mary was born in a small village there in 1945. The family home was little more than a shed with a dirt floor. "No toilet. No running water. No electricity. No nothing," describes Mary. There was a community well, and villagers would manually pump water into jugs and carry them back on their heads. "We had enough water to wash the dishes at night and cook meals and wash up before you went to bed," she recalls.

Mary's uncle emigrated to America when she was a young girl, and notified his family back in the homeland that there were far more lucrative opportunities to be found in his new country. "He let us know that it was much better there, so my mother decided to come too," recalls Mary. "So my mother and I were the pioneers." Mary was 12 years old when she and her mother settled in southeastern Massachusetts in 1958.

"We came from zero, from nothing," shares Mary. "We came to my uncle's house. I went to school without knowing how to speak one word in English. They just kept a paper in front of us with pictures and we had to learn what was the chair, what was the table." She continues, "Why we came here was to better ourselves. Because there, it was a very happy life, very nice, but a struggle because we didn't have anything. There was no money.

We just lived one day after another, making our own gardens and things like that. So we came here just to get ourselves better off."

Mary's mother went to work sewing in the garment mills in Fall River, earning 75 cents an hour, and saved her pay for nine months to be able to bring Mary's father and sister to the United States. Mary didn't have the luxury of staying in school past the sixth grade. "I went from third grade at 12 years old until sixth grade," she notes. "By sixth grade my mother couldn't afford to keep me in school, so I had to get out of school and go to work. So I went to work at 16 years old in the garment industry making clothes."

At age 19, she returned to Portugal on a trip with her parents for her sister's wedding. While she was there, she met Alberto, a 23-year-old electrical apprentice for the government-owned utility company. Alberto followed Mary back to the United States on a three-month visa, and within that time they decided to get married. The couple lived on Mary's income of $27 a week until Alberto was able to get work earning $1 an hour at a yacht-building company.

Within two years, the couple became parents when son Albert was born in 1966. That's when Alberto started taking on other work in addition to his job at the yacht company, where his pay was up to $1.40 an hour. "There wasn't much for us to live on, and he was handy at doing carpentry," Mary says of her husband. "He started telling people what he could do. People would hire him like a second job, like weekends or after work at night. He always had a second job, so we wouldn't struggle."

Son Albert remembers the hours his dad used to keep. "In my early years, my father would come home from working, drop his lunch box, pick up his toolbox, and he'd always have side jobs remodeling houses. Whatever needed to be done that he could find. He'd come home 10, 11:00 at night and then go to work the following morning."

To make ends meet, Mary would take home a sewing pattern from work and make a pair of pants or shorts overnight so she would have clothes to wear to work the following day. Every night she washed her son's cloth diapers and dried them over the stove so she could bring clean supplies to the babysitter where she would drop him the next morning.

Shortly before daughter Theresa was born in 1970, the Lobos managed to scrape together $3,000 to buy a three-family tenement in Fall River. They lived in one unit and rented out the two other apartments, investing a liberal amount of sweat equity to fix up the building. Mary continued working in the garment industry, making $30 or $40 a week.

"I was always a garment worker, making clothes," she reports. "So if there wasn't one job here, I'd go from one job to another and anything that was available. Any overtime, I'd grab any over-time. A Saturday, I'd grab a Saturday. Anything that was available to make a little extra money. We had to work piecework. And when it was piecework, the faster you worked, the more you made."

Mary returned to work within two months of each child's birth. "The poor things," she sighs. "They struggled from two months on, going from babysitter to babysitter." While her husband was out working his second job each night, Mary cared for her children. She made their clothes when they were very young, and cooked and baked, much to their delight. "Albert always loved his sweets. I had to bake him a cake two or three times a week," says Mary. "That's one thing, they ate well and dressed proper. I mean, it wasn't the best of everything, but we didn't go without stuff."

Alberto eventually left the yacht builder to join the carpenters' union, and soon moved on to become a cabinetmaker for a company in southeastern New England. He was promoted to job foreman, and began to travel around the country building fixtures for department stores like Macy's, Bloomingdale's, and

Lord & Taylor. The pay was significantly better working on the road than it had been in the shop.

Mary was in charge of the money. She allocated her own salary toward food and most of the bills, and diligently put her husband's income into savings. "My husband was the breadwinner," she asserts. "But I was a good saver."

When Alberto was on the road, often for months at a time, she would receive his check at home, verify the hours with him over the phone, and promptly deposit it in the bank. She also became an efficient bargain shopper. "I would clip every coupon I could, go to every sale there was," she discloses. "I watch for where the sales are. I don't buy things when I need it, I buy things when they are on sale so when I need it, I have it."

Mary and Alberto were intentionally diligent with their savings because they wanted their children to be able to go to college and have an easier time building a better life. Recounts Alberto, "After the kids were born, I start putting money aside a little bit at a time for the days to come to go to college or to the special school where they give more education. I was saving and saving and saving."

As their savings began to mount, Mary shopped around for high-yield bank CDs. "I would go from bank to bank like it was shopping from store to store, seeing which one is paying the higher rate," she recalls.

In the mid-1970s, while building a porch for a family in town, Alberto was introduced to the homeowner's friend, who was a professional financial advisor. Alberto started to learn about the power of investments from this new friend, and after a while the Lobos grew to develop enough trust that they gave him a minimal sum to invest.

"To tell you the truth, we took a risk," admits Mary. "We started with a little—a few thousand. Then we saw we were making good, go to a little bit more, go to a little bit more." Mary would save up a few weeks of Alberto's pay and shop around for the best available CD, so that when it matured she'd have another chunk to invest with their financial advisor.

By 1978, the couple was able to sell the three-family house and relocate to a single-family home in another New England community. The new house was in good condition so it didn't require any immediate work, and over the years Alberto has remodeled various areas as styles have changed. According to Mary, "The house was $43,000 and we paid cash for it. No debt anywhere. We didn't believe in anything like that. We only believed in saving."

Mary and Alberto always balanced their generosity to their children by teaching them the importance of hard work. "I helped Albert buy his first car. I helped Theresa buy her first car," Mary proudly announces. "The only thing I didn't pay for was their gasoline, but I would pay for their insurance. And Albert had a little bit of money to put down on a house when he got married because at 9 or 10 years old, he was already doing a paper route. And then in the wintertime, he would shovel snow. In the summer, he would cut grass. So I mean I tried to bring them up the way I was brought up, trying to save money."

Even though money was tight, the Lobos splurged from time to time to show their children different parts of the United States, and introduce them to their own homeland, as well. "It's not like we never went anywhere," notes Mary. "We took them to Disney World in their teenage years. We went to Washington. We took them weekends to New Hampshire, to the Cape. We took them to Portugal three times."

The Lobos were able to fulfill the dream of sending their children to college, debt-free. Albert, who was anxious to get a job and earn money, chose to attend a community college, while

Theresa got a degree from a state university. When each of the kids got married, their parents helped them purchase homes. "Our priority was the best for my children," shares Mary. "My children always came first. Was my choice for my children to go to school and once they got out of school, to go to college. And to see them get married and be well in life. That was my priority."

Their son Albert adds, "They both pushed us to better ourselves. They pushed us to have a higher education and better jobs so we wouldn't have to struggle like they did at the beginning."

By investing in instruments like mutual funds and tax-deferred annuities, the Lobos were gratified to watch their money grow. They continued to add to their portfolio over the years, and when their financial advisor retired in 1994, his son, who was also in the investment business, took over responsibility for the account. Within five years, the portfolio's value hit seven figures, and at the height of the market in 2007, it had nearly doubled. It's an astonishing achievement to the couple that literally came from nothing.

"Why I came here was to get myself better off because there I couldn't have what I have here today," confides Mary. "I was very, very poor there. And I'm blessed with what I have here. I didn't have anything in Portugal. So money to me—it's like I feel overwhelmed."

Alberto and Mary have no interest in spending their savings on themselves. Their most sincere, heartfelt satisfaction comes from seeing their children and four grandchildren enjoy the benefit of the money they worked so hard to accumulate and grow. Albert wishes his parents would splurge on themselves once in a while. "We tell them all the time, instead of giving generous gifts to us and your grandkids, why don't you do something for yourselves? And they say they'd just rather give it to us. They feel much happier."

Explains Mary, "What do I have to do? I mean, I've seen. I've gone places. I live in a decent house. We eat well. So I try to share with my children."

The Lobos became concerned that their hard-earned savings could be significantly diminished by taxes or other expenses beyond their control someday, rather than allowing the money to pass along to their family. "My grandkids, I want to see them to be somebody in life," stresses Mary. "I'd like to be able to pay for their college, even if I'm not here. I want them to be successful in life. I don't want them to struggle, like my children are not struggling."

Their financial advisor was able to recommend a strategy to accomplish precisely what the Lobos wished. The couple worked with an estate attorney to create an irrevocable dynasty trust, which is a multigenerational trust designed to preserve an estate as it's passed from generation to generation. Beneficiaries of the Lobos' trust are their children, grandchildren, and potential future generations. They left 35 percent of their portfolio invested, and repositioned the rest to fund a second-to-die life insurance policy, naming the trust as the policy owner. Upon the death of the second spouse, the policy will pay over $3 million tax-free to the trust, which will benefit the family. If the Lobos are no longer living when their grandchildren go off to college, the trust will provide the tuition.

Since the Lobos are able to cover regular living expenses from their pension and Social Security income, they plan to dip into their investment portfolio only under two circumstances. If one or both of them are alive when the grandchildren are ready to pursue higher education, they will use investment funds to pay tuition charges. They will also rely on the portfolio if either or both incur health or welfare expenses that exceed their retirement income.

"I feel grateful," offers Mary. "If I have it, it's because I saved it. We accumulated money by working hard and saving. It wasn't handed to me. It makes me feel good to know that when something, God forbid, happens to us, my kids and grandkids have over $3 million tax-free."

As they had dreamed, coming to America did indeed provide the Lobos the opportunity to make a better life for themselves. They struggled tirelessly so that future generations will be able to get an education and live comfortably. Insuring that their inspiring legacy lives on is the most fulfilling reward this hardworking, forward-thinking couple could ever have imagined.

HARMONIOUS BALANCE

"Life moves pretty fast.
If you don't stop and look around once
in a while, you could miss it."
—Ferris Bueller

HEY BUDDIES,

Creating harmonious balance in your life is a bit like trying to nail Jell-O to the wall. You might actually achieve it but for a fleeting second before some parameter changes, and once again, you're in hot pursuit of the elusive fulfillment of balance.

The most obvious definition of balance is juggling work respon-sibilities and personal interests in a satisfying way, but there are countless other life situations that involve finding a harmonious balance as well. The common denominator is that they all neces-sitate setting clear priorities and making individual choices. Your priorities will continually change throughout life, as your interests, family, work life, and health change, making the challenge of finding balance a never-ending process.

The most basic decision—choosing between what you need and what you want—is fundamentally about balance, as you learned in the previous chapter. When you lack balance in that area and make your wants a priority over your needs, you run the risk of jeop-ardizing your financial equilibrium by incurring debt. But the flip side is becoming such a conditioned saver that you blanch at the thought of a well-planned occasional splurge. One of Dad's greatest challenges, yet most gratifying pleasures, as a professional wealth manager is urging habitually austere older clients to use excess earnings toward a long dreamed-of personal extravagance. He periodically reminds these penny-wise clients that a portion of the savings they worked so hard to build is meant for them to use for enjoyment. With his encouragement, clients have warily acquiesced, indulging in treats ranging from a new computer to an RV to a Disney cruise with the grandchildren to a rented villa in Italy with friends. All were ultimately grateful for the reminder and gentle prodding, and overjoyed with their expenditures because they generated irreplaceable memories.

Money isn't the only asset people sometimes feel a compulsion to preserve. Often they limit the use of something they perceive as quite valuable or rare, or they insist on saving it exclusively for an occasion they deem inordinately special. Maybe they've got a set of fine china that resides inertly in a glass cabinet, or a sports car that is only to be admired in the hermetically sealed garage, or the much-parodied sofa perpetually ensconced in protective plastic, or a splendid dining room that could be rented out for 362 days of the year. Again, it's a balancing act to weigh the pleasure of using these luxuries against the risk of damage or loss, but keep in mind that when you get to the end of your life, there's no prize for the most pristinely preserved set of Royal Doulton or a gleaming Porsche 911 with low mileage. Why save these treasures for a day that may never end up coming, when they can bring happiness to your life on a much more regular basis? As you've learned, life is most assuredly not a dress rehearsal.

In fact, Dorothy J. Gaiter and John Brecher, former wine columnists for the *Wall Street Journal,* actually invented an annual event precisely so people would have a pseudo-occasion to celebrate. They heard so many stories of wine collectors who were saving a cherished bottle for a special occasion that never seemed to come, that in 2000 they declared the last Saturday of February "Open That Bottle Night." Their point was to contrive an event that would encourage readers to make memories by opening a saved bottle of wine alone or with a group of friends, and to inspire that "just because" spirit all year long. "Wine," they write, "like life itself, should be enjoyed."

We've long subscribed to a similar philosophy. To balance the stress and adversity that touches our lives, as it does everyone's, we've made it a practice for our family to celebrate all kinds of successes and milestones, from significant to downright silly. Sure, events like birthdays, anniversaries, and holidays are special occasions and we don't miss an opportunity to gather family and friends and throw a party, but we've discovered myriad excuses worthy of little celebrations almost every day. Losing a tooth, learning to ride a two-wheeler, getting good news, the last day of school, finishing a long project, receiving recognition, the first snow, achieving a goal, a good hair day, the first ripe tomato from the garden, even just plain old Monday. For us, savoring those jubilant moments helps to nourish the soul during the inevitable times when the chips are down.

Sometimes you need to make an effort to balance the different roles in your life. When we first got married, we were balancing the roles of spouses and employees. We both had busy work schedules, so we made it a priority to carve out some time once a week when we put aside our work stresses and had a full-fledged Date Night. Didn't matter whether we cooked at home, went to the movies, had dinner with friends, or split a bucket of fried chicken in a parking lot; it just mattered to both of us that we connected and enjoyed some shared experiences so we didn't each become entirely consumed with work.

Once you boys were born, we found ourselves balancing the roles of being spouses and being parents. Our weekly Date Night became an even more valuable and appreciated escape from sippy cups and Diaper Genies, no matter how exhausted we were, or how unglamorous and unexciting our dates might have been. It's always been a priority for us to make the effort to remember why we fell in love, and as you know, Date Night is a weekly tradition for us to this day.

Then, of course, there's the art of balancing your time. To have even a remote shot at finding harmonious balance with your time, the first—and quite possibly most important—step is to honestly assess what you need and want out of your whole life, not just isolated pockets like your work or your home life, but what truly defines *you*. Until you have figured out your priorities, you can't begin to formulate a way to accommodate everything that matters in your life. It's a given that you need to commit time to your studies now and your job once you enter the workforce full time, but what other activities do you consider to be absolutely essential to your mental, physical, spiritual, and social well-being? Maybe it's spending time with family or riding your bike or volunteering in your community or connecting with nature or cooking or drawing or watching your favorite sports team or worshipping or playing an instrument or gardening. Whatever your unique combination of interests, you need to actively make choices and understand that choices come with consequences. There's no right or wrong, just individual choices and their trade-offs, concessions, and compromises.

So how do you go about fitting everything you want into your life? Again, you need to prioritize your obligations and interests in order of their importance to you. Understand that it's unreasonable to anticipate devoting the same amount of time to each of your priorities. For instance, it's highly unlikely you'll be able to strike an equal balance between work time and personal time, or have a pie divided into eight equal portions for all your interests. But a paraphrasing of the popular "Rocks in a Jar" story in leadership expert Dr. Stephen R. Covey's book, *The Seven Habits of Highly Effective People* (Free Press, 1989), serves as an excellent reminder to make sure you focus on your most important priorities first:

> An instructor at a seminar was giving a lecture on time. At one point, he pulled out a wide-mouthed gallon jar and placed it on the table, next to a platter of fist-sized rocks. One by one, he put rocks into the jar until it was clearly visible that no more would fit.
>
> He asked the group, "Is the jar full?" Everyone agreed that it was. The instructor then reached under the table and pulled out a bucket of gravel, which he dumped into the jar. When he shook the jar, the gravel slid into all the little spaces between the rocks.
>
> This time when he asked the group if the jar was full, they agreed that it probably wasn't. Once again, the instructor reached under the table, this time bringing out a bucket of sand. He started dumping the sand into the jar, where it settled into all the tiny crevices between the rocks and gravel.
>
> When he asked the group, "Now is the jar full?" everyone shouted, "No." The instructor then grabbed a pitcher of water, which he poured into the jar until the sand could absorb no more.
>
> He looked up at the class and asked, "What's my point?" Someone answered, "No matter how full your schedule is, if you try really hard, you can always fit some more things into your life?"
>
> The instructor shook his head. "No," he said. "The point is that if I hadn't put the big rocks in first, I would never have gotten any of them into the jar."

It's up to you to establish boundaries and set limits in order to make time for the activities that are important to you. It used to be easier to leave work at work, and have a clear division between personal time and work time, but those boundaries have blurred due to factors like a competitive global economy; international business that operates 24 hours a day, seven days a week; and advanced communication technology that allows people to work from virtually anywhere.

Taking steps to keep yourself organized and find methods and processes to streamline your productivity are useful ways to free up more personal time. Learning to say "no" is also a powerful time management tool. When you stop burdening yourself with activities you take on out of guilt or a false sense of obligation, you gain more time for the activities that are meaningful to you.

Make every moment count. Don't waste time idly worrying about situations and issues you can't do something about, and remember to get the most out of all you do by being fully present—staying mindfully focused on experiencing the richness of the moment. Disconnect from all the tempting distractions, and pay attention to the nuances of the here and now. How often do you get fed up with Dad for being physically present, but mentally focused on reading and responding to client e-mails?

Life will inevitably throw you curveballs, knocking you off balance. Keeping things in perspective is vital during these times, allowing you to recognize what's really important to you in life. It's almost like a reset button, giving you a renewed opportunity for reflection, personal growth, and refinement of your goals.

Finally, be sure to balance the trivial irritations that you periodically encounter by noticing and appreciating the small joys and simple pleasures that are sprinkled throughout your day, like hearing a great song; biting into a juicy, just-picked strawberry; jumping into a pile of crunchy leaves; listening to the rain on the roof; putting on warm clothes from the dryer; eating freshly baked chocolate chip cookies and a cold glass of milk; getting the best hug;

walking barefoot in the warm sand; snuggling; popping bubble wrap; smelling the perfume of honeysuckle in June; looking at the ocean sparkling in the moonlight; making angels in the snow; singing in your car at the top of your lungs; watching a mama duck leading her precious ducklings; getting the perfect parking spot; gazing at stars. The list goes on and on.

Contentment comes expressly from within, and you are uniquely empowered to manage your lives with harmonious balance so you can enjoy the activities that fulfill you and define you as people.

Someone who has done a magnificent job of discovering and establishing harmonious life balance is Stefani Phipps, and her vibrant, triumphant story is the profile for this chapter. We met Stefani in her capacity as a Managing Director at First Republic Bank, but rest assured, she's not even remotely like the stodgy, conservative banker you're imagining. Her quirky spirit is both endearing and inspiring.

Namaste,
Mama and Dad

STEFANI PHIPPS

What's the best advice you've ever gotten?

If you don't ask, you won't get.

If you were to receive an award, what would you want it to be for?

Putting a smile on the face of everyone I encounter.

Who or what inspires you?

Anyone who follows their dreams and passions without regard for money.

What do you see as the greatest challenge for the next generation of Americans?

Getting with the program that the world doesn't revolve around you.
Keeping human connections despite technology.

What three (famous) people, living or dead, would you invite to your fantasy dinner party?

Oscar Wilde
Dorothy Parker
Noël Coward

Growing up as a second generation Slavic girl in San Francisco during the 1950s and 1960s, Stefani Phipps took to heart the pithy advice printed on one of the little magnets that her mother kept on the refrigerator—"Dare to be different."

Not only did Stefani, a self-proclaimed contrarian, strive to be different from the crowd, but she also managed to create two distinctly divergent inner selves: the hardworking "Work Stefani," an exceedingly successful private banker, and the high-spirited "Life Stefani," one of the most engaged and contagiously captivating characters with whom you could hope to cross paths.

The youngest of three sisters, Stefani attributes her special quirkiness to a unique combination of genetics, good fortune, and birth order. "My parents were very clever to be in California, which is a beautiful place to grow up, a place that celebrates women," she notes. "Even though they themselves were very poor immigrants when they came here, they worked hard enough to attain middle class status in the 50s."

San Francisco, still her home today, played an influential role in shaping two distinct sides to Stefani, as well. "It is a very sophisticated city," she acknowledges. "It also has pockets of immigrants, so that you have the sense of being able to stay with your culture," she adds. "You don't have to assimilate as you would, say, if you went somewhere in the Midwest or in smaller towns where you had to give up your ethnicity. So I literally had dual citizenship growing up—I was an American citizen obviously, but I felt part of the Slavic community." Her grandfather was a priest in the tight-knit community, and Stefani adored learning to cook traditional Slavic dishes with her grandmother.

Being the youngest sibling was particularly formative for Stefani. "As the youngest and as a very strong-willed, high-energy child, my mom gave me more freedom because I fought for it—and because she was tired," she remembers. "I was allowed to take risks. I was allowed freedom and independence as a child, so I could take risks and take responsibility for my failures, because my parents weren't of the type to fix things for me."

Stefani thinks birth order may also explain her eventual path to a career in sales. "Maybe it's being the youngest and trying to vie for attention," she admits. "I had a lot of self-confidence, and I was not afraid to go against the crowd. I loved selling things, but there is a risk in being told, 'No.' And if you are told 'no' and you don't have the confidence or the ability to let it roll off your back," she continues, "you can't do that kind of role."

Stefani was bitten by the sales bug early on. "My grandfather lived with us for a while and he worked at the Dole fruit factory. He'd bring home the old fruit from the day, and I'd go door-to-door and I'd sell the fruit. I also loved selling Girl Scout cookies. That sort of goes into the whole aspect of enjoying people, enjoying everyone's company and enjoying the interactions that I had with everyone."

She instantly recognized she had a gift. "I think you just have that personality or you don't. And if you can be in sales and you can take that risk, you are usually remunerated better," she observes. "So if you go into the sales field, that is where you can make good money."

But while "Work Stefani" was enticed by the idea of cultivating her sales skills, "Life Stefani" was deeply drawn to the arts. She played the piano and double bass from childhood, and considered pursuing a career as a classical musician, until she became disillusioned about the music business. "My bass teacher kept feeling me up at rehearsal. And then I found out that the lead French horn at symphony had gotten there because she had slept with the conductor," Stefani reveals. "And then I found out that so-and-so was an alcoholic, and I realized that there was such a horrifyingly political and nasty aspect to the business, like all businesses. And I wanted to *love* music, not hate it," she reflects. "So I kept it as a side. Decided not to go into that."

As a high school student in the late 1960s in the Bay Area, Stefani was enchanted by the prevalent hippie culture, but true to her contrarian nature, she did it on her own terms. "I started having my season tickets to the symphony, whereas everybody else was going to the Fillmore and doing drugs," she muses. "I refused to do drugs and I refused to listen to rock music. With my season tickets to the symphony, I wore beat-up, old blue jeans that I had hand-embroidered with leather patches. Wore my homemade shoes. No bra. Didn't shave my armpits. Had this wild, woolly 'fro. And that's how I went to the symphony!"

With a passion for music in her heart and soul, Stefani fell in love at age 16 with a talented cellist who played in the same high school orchestra. "He loved the whole ethnic part of me," she says of her young boyfriend, "and we went through the hippie thing together."

She remembers the era being filled with innocence and love. "The whole hippie phase was actually a nice time because it was a very warm and very loving time. It was about community," she reminisces. "We were all together, and we would do things instead of just going out with one person, you would do things in a group. Of course, you are in a group with the orchestra, which is very much working together as a team—so it's like team sports, being in the orchestra."

By the time she entered UC Berkeley in the early 1970s, Stefani was over her hippie phase and had moved on to a new phase in which she was smitten with old black-and-white movies.

"I started doing ballroom dancing, folk dancing. I was president of the Berkeley Folk Dance Club," she recounts. "I was wearing vintage gowns. Katharine Hepburn—I adored her. I saw every Katharine Hepburn movie there was."

While majoring in Serbo-Croatian language and minoring in French at Berkeley, Stefani managed to work full-time as a buyer and manager at the venerable luxury department store, I. Magnin. "I liked working. I never felt like, 'Oh, isn't this terrible? Isn't this hard?'" she shares.

Just out of college, Stefani and her high school sweetheart—the cellist she had met in the school orchestra—married. Her new husband had studied architecture at Berkeley, and was designing high-end homes, so Stefani drew on her sales skills to market the homes, launching her career in luxury real estate sales. She went to work for a boutique firm that specialized in ultra-high-end real estate. "I loved going into these beautiful homes. And I loved helping people find them and fitting them with the houses."

At age 28, Stefani had been with the same man for 12 years, and selling real estate for six, when she had what she calls a little crisis. "I really wanted to do something out of the box. So I said, 'I want to go to the Cordon Bleu, and I've always wanted to.' It was a life dream." And with that, she took off to Paris to spend a year in culinary school, her husband visiting periodically, having just opened his own architectural practice in San Francisco.

"It was a big turning point," she insists. "I loved it. It was the first time I'd ever been away from everyone. I'd lived in San Francisco, had this big family, married my high school sweetheart, went to Berkeley across the bridge. I had travelled with my parents to Yugoslavia to visit cousins, and Europe with my sisters. But I'd never been well and truly alone."

Stefani savored every moment of her culinary education, and she returned to San Francisco to find that the local food scene was booming with the birth of what was being heralded as "California cuisine." More than anything, she longed to go into the food business. "Food was almost more of a passion than music," she confides. "I loved food. Always did. Always, always cooked," she shares passionately. "I had dinner parties through Berkeley. People would come over and I'd have duck dinners. They just loved it. I baked through school, baked to sell stuff. Loved cooking for my family. And I loved the niceties—setting the fancy table and having everything look beautiful and using good china and all that stuff."

But she found herself at a fork in the road, because when she came back to the States, Stefani learned that she and her husband were expecting their first child. "I said, 'I do know one thing, the food business is a killer, and I'm not going to have a child and do a new business at the same time. It's not fair to the child," she recalls. "I knew a lot of players in the food business, but I chose the safe route."

Looking back, however, she's not sure she'd choose the same road again. She resumed selling real estate, having grown accustomed to the lifestyle the income provided. She also figured a real estate career would enable her to manage her work schedule along with raising a family, which eventually grew to include three children.

And then one day in 1992—completely out of the blue—the bottom fell out of Stefani Phipps's life. Her husband of 17 years suddenly announced that he loved someone else, and he moved out, leaving Stefani with their children, ages 10, 7, and 3. "My heart was broken," she laments. "It was absolutely broken and I couldn't understand it. I couldn't understand how we couldn't keep it together and make it work. And he just didn't want to, and that was that. He loved this other woman, and he moved out and left."

The divorce marked the first time in her life that Stefani wasn't in control. "Nothing bad had ever happened to me. Ever, ever, ever," she recounts. "Until then, I had control of everything. Of all my outcomes. I felt very much on top of what happened to my life."

Within six months, life spun further out of control when her three-year-old daughter and her father were both diagnosed with kidney cancer the same week. Stefani subsisted on candy and lattes while running between the floors of the hospital, and lost 40 pounds in six months. Distraught and incensed with life, she says, "I started working out six days a week just to get that anger out. I was never an exercise buff but it was like, 'Oh, this is kind of cool. Oh, look what happens . . . there is one benefit to all of this.'" Exercise was also a way to regain at least a modicum of control over a life that in short order felt like it had been built on quicksand.

Over the course of the next year, her daughter and father both underwent successful treatment, but Stefani's world had been permanently rocked. As her ex-husband withdrew further from her children's lives, Stefani found herself to be a single mother. "And so, I did this on my own—but I didn't really do it on my own because I had my sisters, and I had my mom and my dad, and I had my cousins, and I had my family, and I had my community," she remembers. "I don't know what people do when they don't have their family around. I just couldn't imagine doing this by myself without anybody. That would just be terrifying."

Slowly, as the darkest, most traumatic days began to dissipate, emerged a vibrant, empathetic Life Stefani, whose positive energy and sense of balance become a lasting and encompassing trademark. "From the time I got married through having the kids, I was kind of an overachiever," she reflects. "I was always the school mom, president of this and that, and I felt I had to run the world, and it was in my control. And then, all of a sudden, you sit back and realize, wow, you don't have control over things. So now what do you do?"

The more she disengaged from her role as the wife and mother of the "perfect" family, the more patient and tolerant she found herself becoming. "We had been the perfect family. We had been the perfect couple. I would look around and wonder why everyone wasn't perfect like me. I didn't have time for anyone who wasn't in my inner circle," she shares. Distancing herself from the expectations of that kind of life markedly changed her perspective. "I was a little complacent about that life," admits Stefani. "I think I expected things a little bit too much, and didn't take the time to realize that other people have things in their lives. Now I think about why the person in front of me in the car is driving kind of slowly today. Instead of getting pissed off with him that he is driving slowly, it's like, 'Hmmm, maybe his wife just got diagnosed with cancer.'"

Since that time, Stefani says she has had a powerful sense of daily gratitude for family, for good health, for her life. "It was a big shift for me and I'm grateful for it. I became much more laid back. It's all good. I became so much nicer and more fun. Also, without my ex-husband, I became more of the kind of quirky, off-the-wall, creative, artsy me." She took up playing the harp, and became devoted to dance, both classical and modern—including hip-hop classes. Her favorite artistic outlet has always been cooking, and as a talented home chef, she feels fortunate to live in San Francisco, which she calls "food paradise" because of the extensive variety of resources and diversity of cuisines.

While she continued to sell real estate because it was lucrative and gave her a bit of flexibility to raise her family, the new Life Stefani found her career eminently less rewarding. "I was working with a lot of very spoiled women who I found just tiresome," she scoffs. "You'd take them out to look at houses and they're saying, 'Oh, I couldn't possibly live here. Look at this granite color.' And I'd want to slap them and say, 'What, are you kidding me?!'"

Fortunately, Life Stefani had a profound effect on Work Stefani. Juggling single parenthood and a high-income career took delicate work, because, as Stefani explains, real estate agents are always on call, "like a surgeon," she says drolly. She watched with disdain as other single moms in the office left their kids stranded while they finished a showing or a conversation, and she vowed not to let that happen to her children. She found a splendid solution by adopting the philosophy of an admired San Francisco real estate doyenne who was exceedingly strict about her time. "She was an absolutely tough agent," recalls Stefani. "You'd say, 'I'd like to show this house at 3:00,' and she'd say, 'Sorry, I have appointments. You can see it on Tuesday between 3:00 and 5:00 if your client is interested.' Now your clients don't know if this appointment is a play or a pediatrician's appointment or even getting your hair done. They just know you have an appointment. I adopted that and I made that balance work for me. And if somebody was really serious and they really wanted to see a house, they'd make it work."

Stefani quickly discovered that because of her tendency to network with people who were doing many of the same things she was doing, clients respected her dedication to her children. Proud of her kids and proud of her role as a mom, she would often meet with clients in child-friendly places. "We'd be literally on the hood of the car writing up offers or on the bench of the playground writing up offers or discussing things," she recalls.

Being comfortable with her life and her family gave Stefani the ability to define what kind of people she wanted to work with. "Early on, I decided I'm not going to spend time with jerks. It's not worth any extra money to me," she stresses. "And I carry that through to this day. I only work with people I like, and that's that. And it works out to my benefit."

By 1998, Stefani decided she could no longer bear to spend her days selling real estate. "Every day I did it, I would drive the customers in the car and I was watching my soul fall out the back window," she confides. "So I started putting out the word."

For years, Stefani had been referring clients to First Republic Bank, and she'd sold real estate to some of the bank's top executives. When she started looking for a new career, her reputation for providing extraordinary customer service prompted an acquaintance at the bank to suggest she join their construction lending division. "The bank's attitude was, 'You can teach a sales person credit skills, but you can't teach a credit person sales skills,'" she explains.

Stefani welcomed the opportunity to change careers. Originally focused solely on construction lending, she soon pitched the idea of expanding her scope to include other types of lending, knowing that her vast network of customers and friends had varied borrowing needs. The bank jumped on board. Now, 12 years later, Stefani is a managing director at First Republic, and she handles a broad range of private banking and lending needs.

"I raised the kids. My youngest is in college," she says of her life today. "And now it is all about me and it is a lot of fun. I get to reap the benefits of those connections that I've made throughout life. One of my favorite things in the world to do is connect. I love to connect. Connect the dots. Connect my friends. Connect people I think can enjoy each other or help each other, not just monetarily."

Making connections seems to be the crossroads of the two sides of Stefani, who attributes much of her satisfaction in both work and life to the fact that she spends minimal time in the office. Life Stefani has a whole world outside the office to explore, indulging her passions for family, friends, travel, food, and the arts. "You will never find me in the late afternoon chatting with a work person," she proclaims. "Because as much as I like them, they are not in my will, they are not part of my connections, friends, networking group, cousins, sisters. Maybe we can grab a cup of coffee during the day, but I'm gone. I've got to go try a restaurant or go to a play or whatever," she continues. "It's either got to be fun or make me money. If it's neither of those, I don't spend time on it."

Work Stefani prefers to be out of the office as well, interacting with customers and prospects. "I collect people like they are seashells," she says, "because they are so wonderful. Again, I only work with people I like, and I find them fascinating and fun and there is always something about them I like. It's a pleasure to get to know them. I have so many customers like that, so why would I be at the office talking to the staff—not that there's anything wrong with them. They are very nice people," she insists.

The key to Stefani's interpersonal charm is her remarkable ability to disarm everyone she meets—from the crustiest, most self-important executive to a timid, self-conscious coat-checker at a restaurant. "I just like to bring it down," she admits. "I want people to feel, 'Wow, we can take the masks off now.' We all know the game is out there. We all know what is going on. But we are all in the same place. All of us. There isn't one feeling you have that I haven't had."

Life Stefani is clearly the one driving the bus these days, keeping things in check. "My priorities are people, family, and health. So on a day-to-day basis, I take my health seriously, because without that, forget it, so that is why I eat well and I exercise. And any person who needs me gets my time. I am never too busy. Never too busy." Music and food are also integral to Stefani's joie de vivre. She finds immense joy and relaxation in playing the harp and deep soulful pleasure in cooking and exploring a dazzling array of gourmet cuisines.

Work Stefani wholeheartedly concurs. "I'm lucky that I make a great income doing what I do. But it is not my life. Work does not define my life. I admire those for whom it does define their lives in the sense that it's a passion," she concedes. "But in my job, we're just giving people money. As a matter of fact, it's even worse—we are giving rich people money. It's not a very important job. And that is the perspective. To me, the perspective is health and family, and all else is not terribly meaningful."

— 9 —

KINDNESS & GRATITUDE

"A little consideration, a little thought for others,
makes all the difference."

—Winnie the Pooh

Dear Boys,

Like throngs of other tri-state Jews contemplating the Yom Kippur fast, one evening last fall just before the High Holidays we found ourselves at the appetizing counter at Zabar's in New York City, clutching a ticket that said, "#8." Behind the counter were seven or eight guys in white butcher coats and paper hats, patiently hand-slicing luscious smoked fish for customers, while one counterman was dedicated entirely to announcing numbers and directing the lucky ticket holder to the available slicing station.

We settled in for the wait, and about 10 minutes in, an impatient lady standing near us decided she had had enough, and gave up, kindly handing us her ticket—#98. Within a minute or two, it was our turn, and James, the handsome young fish slicer with piercing blue eyes, waved at us. We greeted him and he asked what he could get for us, and soon he began the tedious process of slicing our order of smoked salmon.

Knowing we would be there for a while—after all, we were going to follow up the salmon with some other scrumptious delicacies—we figured we'd shoot the breeze with James, who has worked at Zabar's for years, and we asked how he had been.

His unexpected answer stopped us both cold.

"Blessed," he replied.

He saw that he had stunned us, and he went on to explain. "I go home to a warm bed. There's food on my table. I have running water and I can take a hot shower. I am blessed."

Indeed, James. Indeed.

How many times a day do you mindlessly ask people, "How are you?" And how many times do you get an empty response like, "Fine," or worse, a miserable reply like, "I'm terrible!" followed by some self-centered whining?

How powerful, gratitude. A simple, truthful, one-word answer became a seminal moment for us. We're *all* blessed, like James. It just depends on how you choose to look at things.

Gratitude is an attitude of deep appreciation and thankfulness for the kindnesses and benefits you perceive yourself as receiving. Practicing gratitude has actually been the subject of recent study, and there is overwhelming evidence that expressing gratefulness has genuine health benefits. Dr. Robert A. Emmons, a professor at the University of California, Davis, has conducted extensive research on the psychology of gratitude, and writes in his 2007 book, *Thanks!: How the New Science of Gratitude Can Make You Happier* (Houghton Mifflin Harcourt, 2007), "Specifically, we have shown that gratitude is positively related to such critical outcomes as life satisfaction, vitality, happiness, self-esteem, optimism, hope, empathy, and the willingness to provide emotional and tangible support for other people, whereas being ungrateful is related to anxiety, depression, envy, materialism, and loneliness."

Additionally, he reveals that cultivating gratitude can increase happiness levels by around 25 percent, and can bring other health effects such as longer and better-quality sleep time, and more time devoted to exercise. Other studies show that people who have been taught to practice being appreciative offer more emotional support to others, and children who practice grateful thinking have more positive attitudes toward school and their families.

We can cultivate gratitude in a variety of ways. Keeping a gratitude journal is a simple and effective means of capturing your blessings, both big and small—from "my peonies bloomed today" or "I had great onion rings at lunch" to "I got accepted to my first choice of college." According to Dr. Emmons, writing in a gratitude journal four times a week for as little as three weeks is often enough to create a meaningful and lasting difference in your level of happiness. As a family, we've tried to set aside weekly time to share things each of us is grateful for, and we know other families who have made this a more regular practice, sharing gratitude daily at the dinner table or at bedtime. Knowing that you will be writing or sharing a few blessings every day or week will encourage you to keep your eyes open for those blessings—almost like viewing life through a gratitude lens.

It's also useful to put your blessings into perspective by recalling circumstances in your life that you felt were less favorable than those you are currently facing, or bringing to mind someone who is or has been in a worse situation than you are. Considering the contrast can be the jolt you need to recognize and appreciate the things you may be thankful for.

Writing a heartfelt personal note thanking someone who has extended kindness, or praising someone who has done a good job or gone above and beyond, is another meaningful way to express gratitude. Some people choose to make an even more profound emotional impact by not only writing a gratitude letter to someone who has had a positive influence on their lives, but actually meeting with that person face-to-face and reading the letter aloud.

When it comes right down to it, there's a glaring lack of gratitude and kindness in our daily interactions. It's always nice to thank people for special things. But it's equally important to appreciate people just for doing what they do every day. "Thank you for being my friend." "Thank you for all you do to teach my children." "Thank you for smiling as you rang up my order." "Thank you for making me laugh." It just brings different energy to your life.

It can honestly be transformational to be generous with your gratitude toward those around you, instead of ignoring, grunting at, or simply tossing a cursory "thanks" to the incidental people you encounter as you go about your daily business. Take an extra few seconds to look people in the eye, smile cheerfully, and give them a sincere "thank you." Even go a step further and add an appreciative comment about what a good job they've done, or how nicely they've treated you, or perhaps let them know you noticed what a beautiful antique pin they're wearing. More often than not, they'll be completely disarmed, and at least smile back—and every once in a while, you'll watch someone light up with a huge grin, as they proudly tell you that the pin was from someone special, or that they've had a rough day and your compliment meant the world to them. Each individual interaction won't change your life or theirs, but cumulatively they make a world of difference. It's almost like starting a chain of kindness.

Speaking of kindness, there's a bittersweet story we wanted to share with you. A family pulled into a gas station in Jacksonville, Florida, one afternoon, on the second day of a long road trip. The dad pumped gas and the mom read the road map in the passenger seat, while the kids, all under age 12, selected and paid for some snacks in the mini-mart. When the dad was finished filling up the tank, he headed into the store to pick up a bottle of water for himself, and as he stepped inside, the cashier stopped him.

"Were those kids yours?" she asked, unsmiling.

"Yes, they were," answered the dad reluctantly, afraid to hear what she was going to tell him next. "Uh-oh. What did they do?"

"They came up to the register, put down their stuff, and said, 'May we buy this, please?'" the cashier recounted.

"Uh-huh . . ." the dad responded, quizzically.

"And when I gave them back their change, they each said, 'Thank you,'" she continued.

"Okay . . ." he commented, still wondering about her point.

"That just never happens anymore," she finally explained. "Kids just don't use manners and say things like 'please' and 'thank you' when they come in here. It was such a nice, refreshing moment!" the cashier exclaimed.

Well, boys, the proud dad was *your* dad and those kids were *you*! The story is bittersweet to us because we're always saddened to learn that polite behavior is the exception rather than the norm. We've received calls from some of your teachers over the years who have wanted us to know that they rarely get the time to make *positive* calls to parents, but that they found it remarkable how consistently helpful, thoughtful, and polite you are at school. Restaurant servers have made a point of commenting on your unusually well-mannered behavior. We never thought we were raising you to have any more appropriate or acceptable manners than anyone else, but obviously we're out of touch if saying "please" and "thank you," smiling, shaking hands, and being appreciative is so abnormal that you are routinely singled out for having what we so boldly assumed to be baseline common courtesy. While that level of politeness and kindness is not always the prevailing behavior when we're at home, we have always expected it of you when we are with others, and we thought most other parents expected the same. Apparently not.

Being kind promotes a sense of connection and community with others, which is one of the strongest factors in increasing happiness. Says Dr. Sonja Lyubomirsky, a professor at the University of California, Riverside, and author of *The How of Happiness* (Penguin, 2007), "Studies from my lab showed that people who commit acts of kindness on a regular basis become significantly happier over time."

Kindness comes in all shapes and sizes. You can lend a listening ear to a friend in need or shovel a neighbor's driveway. Brighten a loved one's day with a phone call or an unexpected favor or a "just because" card. Do a spontaneous act of kindness for a stranger like letting a hurried person cut in front of you in a checkout line or offering to help someone struggling with bags of groceries. Give support to a cause that's important to you, through a financial donation or by volunteering your time, knowledge, energy, and useful skills. But however you express kindness, do it unconditionally, and expect nothing in return.

You have been practicing kindness and thoughtfulness since you were little boys, bestowing treasured handmade cards on family, surprising us with a special breakfast from time to time, cheering up friends who were feeling sad, holding doors for strangers, helping frazzled moms try to calm their unruly toddlers at the supermarket, volunteering your time and giving financial support to meaningful charitable causes.

Ever since you began to receive a weekly allowance, you have made it a practice to set aside a portion for charity. You decide individually how much you wish to allocate, and at the end of the calendar year, you each research and select organizations to receive your donations. Over the years, you've chosen to support a wide range of causes, including organizations that help children and animals, as well as others that champion education, international outreach, disaster relief, and disease research. As you know, part of your charitable fund goes toward the long-standing August tradition we call the "Reiser Brothers' Annual Jimmy Fund Challenge," which we created to combine your love of Boston Red Sox baseball with charitable giving. The Jimmy Fund, which supports cancer research and care at Dana-Farber Cancer Institute in Boston, has been the official charity of the Red Sox since 1953, and each August for a number of years, the Red Sox's broadcasting partners have run a two-day telethon to benefit the fund. During the broadcast of Sox games during those two days, they air incredibly compelling and inspiring interviews with cancer patients and survivors with their families and doctors, as well as family members honoring the memories of patients whose lives have been claimed by the disease. The first year you saw the telethon, you were so deeply touched by the poignant stories that you wanted to find a way to help. Together, we hatched a plan where each of you made a pledge based on a statistic related to the production of the team or a particular player throughout the month of August. Over the years, you've sometimes pledged a certain amount for each Sox home run hit during the month. One of you pledged something for each strikeout by the starting pitchers. One of you made a pledge based on extra-base hits for the month, and another pledged for each RBI. You root even harder for your team during August, knowing that with each on-field success, you'll be helping to make a difference in someone's life.

We are extraordinarily proud of the three of you who have already become bar mitzvahs, as you took it upon yourselves to request that in lieu of gifts, guests instead make a donation to a charitable organization of your choosing. You felt passionately that as fortunate 13-year-olds, receiving gifts would feel over-indulgent, and that the most purposeful gesture to commemorate the occasion would be to make a difference to a cause that was meaningful to you. This was not a custom practiced in our community, but it was personally important to each of you, and brother #4 has already begun considering causes to receive funds gifted in honor of his future bar mitzvah. For the rest of your lives, one of you will feel the satisfaction of knowing that you helped raise almost $25,000 for Susan G. Komen for the Cure (with the largest individual gift being $2,500), and you twins will be proud to know you raised the same amount to benefit the Jimmy Fund at the depth of the 2009 recession.

You have also been generous with your time, volunteering many hours after school at the local public library and as Hebrew tutors at our synagogue, and you are constantly seeking opportunities to lend your energy and skills to community causes that you find significant. Perhaps you've learned the importance of community service from Mom, who dedicates much of her time to volunteering on boards and committees at your schools, at our synagogue, and with other community organizations. Mom grew up watching *her* parents and grandparents serve the community, and especially admired her mom—your "Mimi"—who taught her the value and fulfillment of volunteering.

Mimi was an exemplary model of a committed community leader. Throughout her all-too-short lifetime, she made a difference in the lives of the young and the elderly. She cofounded an organization called Volunteers in Cranston Schools, which coordinated parent and community volunteers for the public schools in her city, and she served as a leader and board member of numerous organizations and institutions, including her synagogue and other Jewish community service organizations. Active for over 30 years with the Jewish Federation of Rhode Island, Mimi took on a variety of volunteer and lay leadership roles, chairing educational programs and fundraising events, and working on committees that determined fund allocations and reviewed endowment grant requests. She was honored in 1987 for her commitment to the local Jewish community as she received the Merrill L. Hassenfeld Leadership in Community Service Award. With her compassionate concern for Rhode Island's Jewish elderly population, she was an active board member of the Jewish Seniors Agency for many years, and eventually served as the organization's president. You no doubt remember that she was integral in the planning and development of the Phyllis Siperstein Tamarisk Assisted Living Residence, and we know you cherish the photo of three generations of our family—including all of you as little boys—donning hardhats at the groundbreaking ceremony for the facility. In 2005, just months before she succumbed to breast cancer at age 63, Mimi was presented the Maurice Glicksman Leadership Award by the Jewish Seniors Agency, which recognized her exceptional leadership as well as qualities such as vision, courage, and the ability to inspire and motivate others. Said a fellow community leader with whom Mimi worked closely, "She was unstinting in the giving of her time, even as she juggled taking care of an aging and ill mother and enjoying and helping with her grandchildren. The Jewish community was blessed by her attention and her service to it."

You are blessed to be surrounded by other resplendent examples of people who live their lives with a kind and grateful attitude, and we share two profiles—featuring three of our favorite people in the world—to personify these interconnected virtues. The first profile highlights our treasured lifelong friends, Linda and Dan Kortick, who graciously extend their altruism to a number of organizations and institutions to which they feel a connection of gratitude. Giving back to the community is a priority to the Korticks, who are raising their daughter to think and act compassionately toward the world as well. Your beloved aunt, Meredith Fried, is the subject of the second profile. As you know and warmly appreciate, "Auntie Mere" is adored for her unceasing kindness to family, friends, and strangers alike. Her perpetually radiant smile and cheerful demeanor inspire benevolence in nearly everyone she meets, and as a cancer survivor, she has found a particularly meaningful way to express her strong personal gratitude. We feel endlessly grateful to have these three special people in our lives.

Blessings,
Mama and Dad

LINDA KORTICK

What's the best advice you've ever gotten?

Believe in miracles.

If you were to receive an award, what would you want it to be for?

The "Random Acts of Kindness" Award, where I would be remembered not for
one big thing, but rather for a lifetime of smaller, simple acts.

Who or what inspires you?

My daughter.

**What do you see as the greatest challenge for the next generation of
Americans?**

Complacency.
A decaying world.

**What three (famous) people, living or dead, would you invite to your
fantasy dinner party?**

Jesus Christ
Martin Luther King, Jr.
Gandhi

DAN KORTICK

What's the best advice you've ever gotten?

Don't crash.

If you were to receive an award, what would you want it to be for?

For never having gotten an award.

Who or what inspires you?

My daughter.
Anybody who performs at the top of their game. It doesn't necessarily mean professional, just someone who performs to the best of the ability—whatever their ability is—and gives it their all, whether in business, sports, or whatever it is.

What do you see as the greatest challenge for the next generation of Americans?

Navigating through an increasingly complex world and being able to sort through information and identify what's relevant.

What three (famous) people, living or dead, would you invite to your fantasy dinner party?

My daughter's future husband and his parents
The Founding Fathers of the United States

Y ou couldn't ask for more gracious or generous lifelong friends than Linda and Dan Kortick. But their generosity extends far beyond their network of personal friends to a wide scope of fortunate strangers whose lives are touched in immeasurable ways by the good-hearted couple.

The Korticks live outside New York City, where Dan is a managing partner at The Wicks Group, a private equity firm, and Linda, a former corporate attorney, has the rewarding privilege of focusing on raising their daughter, Genny, now 10. They both gladly share their time and expertise giving back to the community.

"I think it's a fundamental obligation to give your time or your resources as just a member of society," emphasizes Linda. "I think there shouldn't be a question as to do you or don't you. The question is how much you can do."

Dan goes further. "It's not about the money. I mean, the money is obviously helpful, but whether you make $10,000 a year or $10 million, I don't think the obligation is any different to just be a giving person." He continues, "I think everybody has an obligation to do something that's meaningful to them. And that might mean $10 to one person and $10,000 to another. But the level of satisfaction to each of those people is going to be the same."

Linda feels especially fortunate to be able to contribute support and service to a number of charitable causes. "Because Dan was able to take a job that allowed me to stay home, I can give more time. If I was working 10 hours a day as a lawyer in the city, I wouldn't have that opportunity." She adds, "There are so many charitable organizations we support, but when the rubber meets the road, it's not just the support of them, it's service to them as well. Sure, we write a check to the envelopes that come into the mailbox, but unless you have sort of a personal involvement with them and get to know their organization, that's where you really feel you're giving, and you're able to be a productive part of that organization."

Particularly close to Linda's heart is the local chapter of the Boys & Girls Club, a national organization that serves at-risk young people by providing programs and services to promote and enhance the development of boys and girls by instilling a sense of competence, usefulness, belonging, and influence. "They help children with programs after school, with everything from education to daycare to just providing meals," reports Linda.

Her fond affinity for the Boys & Girls Club stems from what the organization meant to her late father. The youngest of four children, Linda's dad lost his own father in 1936 when he was just two years old, leaving his mom to raise the family on her own during the Great Depression. She went to work as a house cleaner, and left Linda's dad each day at the Boys Club of New Haven, the organization's founding club, established back in 1873.

"My dad would go there every day as a little boy, and then once he was school-age, he would go after school," shares Linda. "And it's there that he learned very important and fundamental things about service, education, and opportunities in life." She continues, "He became a swimmer and he would swim for the Boys Club, as they called it then. He ended up becoming the Connecticut state champion swimmer as a result, and it opened up a lot of doors for him. I even have pictures of him back when he was a tiny little skinny thing, in like 1940, standing there with the Boys Club swim team."

According to Linda, her father talked with extraordinary gratitude about what a profound impact the Boys Club had on him. "It was a place he needed to go," says Linda. "And there are so many people out there today that need a place like that. Even though I had never gone to a Boys & Girls Club, I had heard my dad talk about it. And so, that's why I have a special kinship to that particular organization. I've always felt I've had sort of a connection to it."

Linda also works to help raise funds for Open Door Family Medical Centers, walk-in clinics that provide quality health care and human services at affordable prices to an economically disadvantaged population in Westchester County. She strongly supports the educational component that patients get at Open Door in addition to treatment. "They teach prevention and education, which is critical," she notes. "Things like why immunizations are important. Why you need to have your bloodwork done. Why you need to have PAP smears and breast exams."

One of Linda's most rewarding volunteer experiences is with her local school district, where she serves as a parent advocate on the committee for preschool education for children with disabilities. In that role, she offers support for parents who are beginning to navigate the unfamiliar, often daunting process of requesting special education services for their child from the school district and the state. Approaching the school committee for services that are in the best interest of your own child can be frightening, particularly for parents who may not have life or work experience that has required them to be proactive and persistent.

"The process can be very intimidating for someone who's not used to it," she explains. "Genny started that process when she was 18 months old. And with my legal background, I felt very comfortable in that forum. The regulations and statutes can be overwhelming. And so I help other parents that are entering the process and continuing through it to help guide them."

Dan elaborates, "When you're the parent of a child with special needs—no matter how major or minor—it's an emotional issue. While school districts are required to provide services, at the end of the day, they've got a tight budget."

It's exclusively up to each family to decide whether they wish to take advantage of Linda's emotional and informational support. Dan contends, "Someone needs to be an advocate for that kid and that family. And it's not going to be the school district. Sometimes parents can be good advocates, sometimes they can't."

Linda adds, "I've sat on the committee for a number of years. Sometimes parents call, sometimes they don't. But it's very, very rewarding, especially when you see the child receive services, and as the years go on, you see that they really benefit from them." She goes on, "I feel like I can be a part of something bigger than myself–that I've touched a life, even in the most separated way. I feel that it does make a difference."

As for Dan, despite his demanding business schedule, he remains tirelessly committed to his volunteer work at Blythedale Children's Hospital, a facility in Westchester that is dedicated exclusively to the diagnosis, care, and treatment of children with complex medical and rehabilitative needs. The Korticks were initially introduced to Blythedale when their daughter received outpatient services there as a toddler, but ironically Dan didn't reconnect with the hospital until several years later when he was involved in fundraising work with United Jewish Appeal (UJA) in New York City.

"What I found in working with UJA, is that similar to the United Way, they provide support to different agencies, as opposed to actually doing a lot of the work with the organizations. They help make sure the money gets where it needs to be," explains Dan. "I wanted to get closer to where the action is. It's not just about writing a check and helping them fundraise and attending events. That's all fun, but at the end of the day, I want to be where you're actually touching and feeling what's happening with all that money that gets raised." As it turned out, Blythedale was one of the agencies that received support through UJA, and Dan was able to circle back and get more involved directly at the hospital instead of giving indirect financial support through another organization.

"It's been five years that I've been working very closely at Blythedale," offers Dan. "I'm in touch weekly with the organization, through e-mail, voicemail, talking with people there. We support every event that they do. We'll help them in any way."

Dan cochairs Blythedale's annual golf and tennis event, which he explains is purposely more interactive and educational than strictly a social fundraising opportunity. "The event is as much an outreach to the community to get people to learn about the hospital," he reports. "It's a chance to really capture people and not just get them in a room to have cocktails and have an auction and then they leave."

Having a firsthand view of the difference that financial generosity makes is especially meaningful to Dan. "Why am I giving my time and resources to Blythedale? Because I get to see the people who are the beneficiaries of what they are doing there," he confides. He tells the story of a mother whose son received extensive treatment at Blythedale as an inpatient for months following a serious bike accident that resulted in a traumatic head injury. The family's experience at the hospital was exceptionally positive, and several years later the young man was able to graduate from high school with his class and was accepted to an excellent university. The mother has returned the family's immeasurable gratitude to the hospital by actively serving on its board of trustees, as Dan emphasizes, "Not because she has the financial resources to do it, but who better to be an advocate for the hospital than someone who's been a direct beneficiary of it? To be the beneficiary of generosity, that's the best lesson you can have."

Recognizing the benefits and privileges of his high school and college education, Dan is a fervent supporter of both institutions, choosing to direct his gifts specifically to scholarship funds. "From a giving perspective, I've given back to Hobart every year since I graduated," he reveals. "I guess I think of college as more of a luxury than high school, so I want my contributions to go to scholarships because that's giving kids an opportunity who otherwise wouldn't have that opportunity." He's also involved in helping set strategic direction for his alma mater, to ensure diversity among the college's future student body. "There are other schools in our peer group with endowments five, ten times what ours are," he offers. "You read about it every day now that schools are forced to make acceptance decisions based on whether the kid can afford to go there. And if you say that you're only going to accept kids who can afford to pay full boat, you're going to have a different student body than you would if the school was able to help." He continues, "So we think about how we're going to do more with less, or how we'll get more but stay true to our values."

Although he doesn't have quite as lengthy a donor history at the private high school he attended, Dan says his appreciation for his education became much more profound once he became a parent himself. "It's not until your child goes to school that you realize how big an impact the school has on your kid," he suggests. "You don't realize how your schools have shaped you until you see it through the eyes of your child. While I didn't give them credit for it at the time, the school did provide me an environment that has certainly allowed me to go to college and get a job. They certainly had an impact."

Dan has recently been involved in a yearlong fundraising effort for his high school in honor of his class' 25th reunion, but he also serves longer term on the school's investment committee, which is responsible for managing the school's endowment. "I've got something to offer," he says. "They certainly have a staff and they hire people to help manage the endowment. But they also recognize that they have an alumni base that has capabilities and opinions that can help them out."

Between Linda and Dan's schools and the school their daughter, Genny, attends, Linda calculates that the family provides support and service to eight educational institutions. "Financial support is a constant," she notes. "But what separates the wheat from the chaff is when you start giving your time and opinions about things. Giving service. You try to say yes as much as you can, because even if it's just a little, it's better than nothing."

"At the end of the day, I'd say we support anybody who asks," admits Dan. "Part of our giving philosophy is to have a connection to the organization, and part of the philosophy is trying not to say no."

Dan remembers trying to explain to his daughter the delicate balance between saying yes and saying no. He and Genny have an annual tradition of spending the day before Thanksgiving on a father-daughter adventure in New York City. "During the holidays there's always more of a giving spirit in the city," he describes. "Two or three years ago, we were walking down Madison Avenue and a homeless woman came up to Genny and me, asking for some help. I don't know whether we were in a rush or what, but we kind of blew her off," he recalls. Half a block later, Genny asked her dad why they didn't help the woman. He tried to explain that it's just not possible to help everybody. "I said, 'You'll run out of time in your life, you'll run out of money. You just can't do it,'" he recounts. And then as he looked down at his young daughter and saw the compassion in her eyes, he had a change of heart. "I said to her, 'You know what, let's go.' And we turned around and went back and gave her some money."

Dan says he's pretty certain there was never a moment when he sat his daughter down and explicitly taught her about charitable responsibility. "It's not like the birds-and-the-bees talk, where your parents sit you down and say, 'Here's how it works,'" he acknowledges. So one day he point-blank asked Genny how she had learned about generosity and giving. "Her answer, almost word-for-word was, 'Aren't you supposed to think about other people before you think about yourself?'" He wondered how she had learned that philosophy. "Well, Dad," replied Genny. "I see you and Mom doing it, and that's just the way you are." Dan realized what a significant impact the simple mention of his daily schedule had on his daughter. "I'll tell her that I've got to leave early today because I've got a meeting at Blythedale, or I'm going to be home late tonight because I've got a dinner with the president of Hobart. She sees that it's just part of my day," he figures. "It was the same for me growing up. My parents would say, 'Oh I had lunch today with so-and-so from the temple' or 'I had a meeting with so-and-so from the YMCA' or whatever it was."

Linda thinks teaching people generosity begins with providing them the opportunity to give. She describes how she collects all the donation requests that land in the mailbox at the holiday season, and during Hanukkah, she and Dan give Genny the opportunity to sort through the envelopes and select a different recipient for each of the eight nights. "Inevitably, it will be one that she has some sort of personal connection to," maintains Linda. "So it will be the ASPCA because she has dogs. It will be Celebral Palsy of Westchester because she has cerebral palsy. It will be the Bretton Woods Adaptive Ski Program because she skis with them," she notes.

The second part of the lesson, according to Linda, comes in providing an opportunity to get to know the organization, which often makes people more inclined to want to help. "So if it's a soup kitchen, you go to that soup kitchen and serve," says Linda. "If it's Blythedale, you go and read books in the library to kids who are unable to. That's part of the education," she emphasizes.

"I think then people truly have a passion. They understand that the money is going somewhere. It exists. You can touch it, feel it—it's tangible."

Linda believes that the act of giving is self-perpetuating. "I think people need to be given an opportunity to give," she reasons. "Because once you make the choice to do it, you feel good about yourself. You feel proud and you feel that you're making a difference in someone's life. Your outlook on the world is better, and it just grows from there."

MEREDITH FRIED

What's the best advice you've ever gotten?

If you have ownership, you must take ownership.
You've got to show up.
You have two ears and one mouth—use them in those proportions.
Don't go to dinner with bad putters.
Insanity is doing the same thing over and over and expecting different results.

If you were to receive an award, what would you want it to be for?

A job well done.

Who or what inspires you?

My kids.

What do you see as the greatest challenge for the next generation of Americans?

Being able to have a strong work ethic when they are a generation that's been built on immediate gratification.

What three (famous) people, living or dead, would you invite to your fantasy dinner party?

My mom
Nana
Grandpa

Some people collect vintage postcards, others collect auto-graphed baseballs. Meredith Fried collects friends.

To know the Boston-area wife and mother of two is to admire an exceedingly cheery, warmhearted, compassionate woman in her early 40s. She's the kind of person you genuinely feel blessed to know, bringing a vibrant, positive energy and loyal supportiveness to all whose lives she touches.

"Meredith's admirable traits are quickly visible to all who get to know her," says a longtime friend. "And those of us lucky to count her among our good friends see the same things magnified."

Shares another, "Meredith is one of those people who is so easy to talk to, and she makes you feel as though you are all that matters."

And another adds, "I always leave her feeling that I have been able to spill my guts, and she hasn't told me a thing!"

Even casual acquaintances quickly sense her unique extra-ordinariness. As one comments, "I've probably had less than 10 personal interactions with Meredith in my life, but she leaves you wanting more of what she has to offer," he admits. "It's like she knows life's little secret, and she's giving enough that she just might share it with you."

Perhaps that indefinable quality that Meredith's friends so greatly admire is her innate ability to be a mirror for them. By listening with a caring ear, and gently asking guiding questions, Meredith reflects back at friends the image of the best person they can be, and inspires them to be that person.

"I listen to people and guide them to come to their own conclusions," she claims. "I'm not there saying, 'Yes, that's good,' or 'No, that's bad,' I validate that just making a decision is impor-tant." She calls the technique "guided discovery"—and claims she learned the term in her career as a sales training consultant. But surely she had the gift long before she had ever heard of sales training, which is inevitably why she has countless friendships that date back to birth.

A key to holding up the mirror is being a world-class listener. "There's a difference between listening with the intent to respond and listening with the intent to understand," she explains. "And I do a lot of listening with the intent to understand. I think for some people, it's nice just to have an objective person to listen."

She adds, "It helps people feel valued that you're spending time to listen to them. It gives people time to reflect as they are speaking, helping them validate their thoughts and feelings. Also, when you listen to somebody, it's showing them respect."

According to Meredith, asking good questions is an active part of listening, and it invites people to open up. "It's asking open-ended questions and it's keying in on things that you hear that it seems like people want to talk about," reveals Meredith. "So, it can be words or topics that they bring up or it could be the things they're *not* talking about that you bring up. People will lead you."

Asking questions has always been part of Meredith's makeup. "I'm an analytical person, so I'm an information gatherer by nature," she admits. "I'm all about the information. I like to listen to what's going on."

When a friend approaches her with problems or complaints, instead of offering comments or advice, Meredith holds up a mirror by repeating back what the person has said. "When you hear your words from somebody else, it either helps you reframe things, it reinforces your feelings, or makes you realize that you sound sort of ridiculous," she observes.

Often, just listening and helping friends own and refine their thoughts is enough to empower them to take a step they've been afraid to, or come to a solution that had been alluding them.

"It's not necessarily the response I give that helps people or draws them to me, I just talk through the issues with them," says Meredith. "It gives people the liberty to speak and explore, and that, in and of itself, is valuable for people. It allows them to unlock different approaches that they might consider."

In addition to her outstanding listening skills, Meredith also shares a contagious positive energy about life, which tends to make people leave the interaction with a good feeling. "I think a lot of it is because I'm a good listener, but also my attitude comes through," she suspects. "People reflect that attitude. In general, I'm a happy person. I'm an optimistic person. I'm a glass half-full person."

But mind you, she's no Pollyanna. "If a friend comes to me and says, 'My job sucks,' I won't say to them, 'Oh, but at least you have your health,'" she emphasizes. "But, in general, I don't lay people with problems because I don't feel like I have a whole lot of problems. So people don't leave me feeling like they have the weight of the world, because I'm not laying anything on them."

She continues, "In addition, if they're talking about something that's going on with them, I'm taking it and I'm dispersing it and helping it and bringing up some other things. So, it's not that they're coming to a conclusion about anything in particular, but I think I help lighten the load, or help people come to understand why their load is not so heavy."

Says a longtime friend, "Meredith finds the silver lining in almost everything. I have very few friends who are consistently like that, and know no one else in our generation with such a straightforward outlook on life."

Meredith also has a flair for making people feel comfortable looking at themselves in the mirror. She exercises steadfast restraint and the diplomacy to reserve judgment, while purposely giving people the opportunity to highlight their accomplishments and achievements. "It's just making people feel competent in what they do," she asserts. "It's recognizing in people the things that they want to be recognized for. I ask them about things that are important to them because that's what makes them feel good. If you get people to talk about things that they feel good about, they leave feeling good about themselves."

Humble to the core, Meredith is quite matter-of-fact about her own life. "I think a lot of my attitude is that the things I can't control, I generally don't worry about." The things she *can* control, on the other hand, she chooses to manage with as many facts as she can get her hands on, and a gracious smile on her face. And perhaps the greatest inspiration for friends to discover their best selves comes from seeing Meredith approach life—because her attitude has turned out to be life-saving.

Shortly after her mother was diagnosed with breast cancer and identified as a carrier of the BRCA-1 gene mutation in 2004, Meredith contemplated making the decision to find out whether she also had the gene, which predisposes the carrier to up to an 85 percent risk of developing breast cancer, and a 55 percent chance for developing ovarian cancer.

"When my mother was diagnosed at stage IV and then we found out she had the gene—and had she known she had the gene, it probably would've been caught earlier—to me, it was a no-brainer," she emphasizes. "I knew early notice would really be useful in this situation. Having information and being able to act on it seemed like a fairly easy thing to do to be able to decrease the risk of something that's so potentially deadly."

Meredith had a clear idea of what she would do if she tested positive for the gene. "My inclination was that if I were positive, I would, at the recommended age or around that time, have mastectomies and oophorectomies," she reports.

In February of 2005, eight months pregnant with her second child, Meredith learned that she indeed carried the gene. She listened openly and diligently to the genetic counselor who revealed her results, and soon after was invited to participate in a focus group at Dana-Farber Cancer Institute in Boston for women who were gene positive but had not had a cancer diagnosis—an invitation she eagerly accepted.

"I was interested in being part of that group because I figured it was an opportunity to hear more about things and meet people who had been in that situation," she recalls. "I wasn't in a position to do anything surgically at that time, but it was just the opportunity to learn and find out more about the gene itself, about the potential treatment options, and about the community of gene-positive people."

Meredith and her family experienced the poignant bitter-sweetness of life just a short time later. The very week Meredith's daughter was born in March of 2005, her mom began radiation treatments for the cancer, thought to have been under control, but tragically found to have metastasized to the brain. The new baby brought a joyful counterpoint to the heartbreaking decline in Meredith's mother's health throughout the rest of 2005. Her mom and daughter were able to share three precious seasons getting to know each other, before her mom lost her courageous battle five days before the new year.

As Meredith's daughter approached her first birthday several months later, Meredith wound down her breastfeeding routine, and mindful of her genetic predisposition, immediately took the opportunity to have a baseline breast MRI. The results were almost unthinkable. The MRI had detected a microscopic tumor, and a subsequent biopsy confirmed a cancer diagnosis.

Information and an upbeat attitude enabled Meredith to move quickly through the next steps.

"I was already immersed in it. I had already been through it with my mom, I had already known for a year that I had this gene, and I had been part of a focus group," she reasons. "I already had an oncologist, and we were kind of looking for it, so when we found it, it was surprising but not shocking. It wasn't out of the blue."

Optimistic and resolute, Meredith followed some of her own favorite advice: You are your own best advocate. She called and followed up with doctors, and again embarked on an information gathering quest. Knowing that her mother's illness had followed a non-conventional metastatic course, Meredith insisted on having body and brain scans as a precautionary measure, even though the tests were not normally indicated.

"I was very grateful that I wasn't top of the priority list for my oncologist," she shares. "I wasn't a 38-year-old woman with stage IV cancer, I was 38-year-old woman who was gene-positive, who had this teeny little thing that they were going to take out. But I kept calling and calling back to get a full body scan and a brain scan. And so they scheduled it," she recounts.

Thankfully, the scans showed that the cancer was contained to the original spot in the breast. The mastectomies, oophorectomies, and reconstructive surgeries had already been on Meredith's horizon, as she had planned to undergo eventual prophylactic procedures. What she hadn't consciously considered until that time was the need for cancer treatment.

The oncologist outlined several possible treatment options, and Meredith, knowing her family history, chose the most aggressive: a course of chemotherapy, which she endured during the summer of 2006. Even with the expected debilitating side effects, Meredith's positive outlook shone through. With a wink and a grin, she shared with friends that the upside of losing her hair was that she no longer had to struggle with taming her curls, especially in the brutal heat and humidity of a Boston summer.

Now, more than four years later, Meredith enjoys good health, treasures her beautiful family, and rocks a spunky short hairdo, which she says she never would have discovered had she not lost her hair. Although she doesn't consider the way she handled her cancer challenge to be courageous, she accepts the idea that her approach may seem inspirational to others. "My personal way is that I don't get all wound up about things I can't impact, and I think sometimes people see that in me and they respect and admire it," she concedes. "It's liberating for certain people because they say, 'Wow, if she can go through that and not think it's a big deal, then what do I have to complain about?' But that's not anything I do purposely, it's just my hard-wiring."

Meredith also spends much of her spare time—when she's not caring for her children, lending a comforting shoulder to friends, or running her sales training consulting practice—volunteering as a mentor to women who are gene-positive or have received a breast cancer diagnosis.

"For me, mentoring is a way that I can give back," offers Meredith. "I'm happy to share, and I like helping people. I think I understand the importance of listening, and I appreciate the fact that people have been there to do that for me, so it's one of those pay-it-forward things."

In addition to linking with women formally through organizations like Facing Our Risk of Cancer Empowered (www.facingourrisk.org) and Sharsheret (www.sharsheret.org), Meredith also gladly speaks with peers referred through friends.

"When people call me and say, 'I have a friend who was just diagnosed, will you talk to her?' I say, 'Of course.'" she explains. "Partly because people did it for me, but also because I don't mind talking about it. It doesn't bring me to a bad place. It's a very fulfilling thing to do."

She continues, "The goal of mentoring is to provide a person someone they can connect with. Mostly what these women need is just an ear. They either need to talk through things themselves, or they just want somebody to listen, or to yell at, or to yell with."

Meredith says she tries to offer helpful suggestions and guidance based on what she learns the woman is looking for, but as a mentor, she is never supposed to give specific advice. Rather, she shares information and personal experiences so these women are empowered to make decisions about their own courses of treatment. "You're giving people information to empower them to be successful at what they need to do," she describes. "When I talk to people in a mentoring role, I try to encourage them to ask more questions of their doctors, to go out and get additional resources if they're looking for it, and I certainly commend them for taking the initiative to tap into whatever network they've already tapped into."

Whether she's holding up the mirror as a mentor or as a good friend, Meredith finds joy in sharing her life with others. "I just like being with people. It's energizing. It's inspiring," she confesses. "When you help people reflect, that helps them get a different perspective. I don't purposely inspire people, nor do I think it's anything I say that inspires people. In fact, I don't do anything to unlock things for people other than opening up the door and encouraging them to come through."

Who wouldn't want a friend that inspires you to be your finest self?

10

COURAGE &
LIVING WITHOUT
REGRETS

"Twenty years from now you will be more
disappointed by the things that you didn't do than
by the ones you did do.
So throw off the bowlines.
Sail away from the safe harbor.
Catch the trade winds in your sails.
Explore. Dream. Discover."

—Mark Twain

Greetings Gents,

The concepts of courage and living without regrets are as delicately interconnected as the earth and the sun, and one of the most compelling ways we could think of to explain the intricacy of these life-changing virtues is by sharing a profoundly personal story.

Like your aunt who was profiled in the last chapter, Mom, too, learned that she carried the gene mutation that predisposed her to a much higher risk of developing breast cancer. As you may remember, given her genetics and family health history, Mom made the choice to reduce her risk significantly by undergoing prophylactic mastectomy surgery. Many friends considered Mom's choice to be courageous, however Mom vigorously dispelled that ascription, instead considering her choice to be just good, prudent sense. She perceived the risk of *not* doing the surgery to be far greater (and far stupider!) than the risk of doing it, thereby removing any intimation of courage.

It was the choice that our family was inspired to make *after* Mom's surgery that could be considered courageous. When Mom opened her eyes in recovery, 11 hours after being wheeled into the operating room, alone and deeply grateful to have come through the surgery—and that someone had put her glasses on her face—the first thing she saw was a clock at the nurses' station across from her bed. It read 7:10. It's a time Mom says she will never forget, because it was the first minute of the rest of her life.

Although her own mother's death at age 63, just 14 months earlier, had raised the headline, "Life Is Short—Choose to Live the Life You Want," the experience of her surgery put it in all caps and flashing bright lights.

Mom had long measured opportunity using the "regret factor"—as in, "If I pass up this opportunity will I regret it?"—but when she awoke in the hospital that evening, she felt so boldly empowered with courage, that she promised herself that she would approach the rest of her life by taking supreme advantage of her newfound strength, rather than losing momentum and settling back into the same comfortable but rather safe life.

Admittedly, life wasn't so terrible where we were. Quite the contrary, as a matter of fact. Our blessings were abundant. We were healthy, we were happily married, we had you four wonderful boys, we had been living in a beautiful waterfront home that we had built, and we had loving family and treasured friends living nearby. But by the same token, there were also some issues that weren't completely fulfilling to us. Mom, who was the fourth generation of her family to be living in the same community, had begun to wonder about life beyond the borders of the small state of Rhode Island. After many years with the same firm, Dad had become disheartened by the corporate politics in his branch office. The state's income tax structure was punitive, our local real estate taxes were absurdly high, and because the local schools didn't offer all the opportunities we wanted for you, we would soon be footing the bill for four private school tuitions.

The new energy that Mom harnessed instantly gave her a different perspective on life. The week before her surgery, we had received an invitation to a worthy fundraising event three hours away in Manhattan. Mom spent a few minutes imagining how much she would enjoy being able to go to New York to attend that event and others like it on a regular basis. But she quietly dismissed the fantasy, knowing it would involve an expensive overnight stay in the city, plus the tall order of finding a brave and responsible soul willing to stay at home with you boys.

The week *after* her surgery, however, as she was flipping through that week's *New Yorker*, she paused longingly, like she did every week, at the "Goings On About Town" pages, which describe the many fabulous cultural and entertainment events that are taking place that week in and around the city.

"*That's* what I want in my life!" she thought. "I want to be able to participate in so many of these things." She immediately realized that years later she would look back at her life with regret and disappointment if she didn't at least try to make that happen.

"What would you think of moving somewhere closer to New York?" Mom asked. Intrigued, Dad thought it was quite an interesting idea to consider. Staying in Rhode Island—comfortable, safe, yet stagnant—wouldn't fulfill what both of us really wanted from life. And we pictured ourselves someday rocking on the glider on our mahogany deck overlooking Narragansett Bay, wondering what could've been.

So 10 days post-surgery, we piled you guys into the car for our memorable exploratory trip to Westport, Connecticut, even though we knew not a soul who lived there. On paper, the beach-side town met all our criteria: top-rated public schools, a sizeable Jewish population, proximity to New York City, and within a two-hour drive to visit grandparents. Although Mom was propped up with pillows in the passenger seat, still sporting surgical drains and glued to a strict mega-antibiotic schedule, we were all enchanted by what we found. Things quickly fell into place, and we moved to our new community just three months later. As you know, it's a decision we have never second-guessed. You all transitioned easily and eagerly to your new schools, made wonderful friends, and quickly made a name for our family at our new synagogue.

Dad arranged to transfer within his company to a different branch, discovering tremendous professional opportunities that had been wholly unattainable in Rhode Island. Mom focused her energies on volunteering at educational and Jewish organizations in our new community. Our real estate taxes wound up being significantly lower for the same size home, and as it happened, the already exorbitant taxes on our old Rhode Island house nearly *doubled* within a couple of years of our selling it. Best of all, we immediately began taking full advantage of our proximity to New York City, going to shows and concerts, visiting museums, and dining at a dazzling variety of the city's remarkable restaurants—opening up a world of enriching cultural experiences for you boys on a regular basis. In all respects, the move has fulfilled our wishes and dreams many times over, and has allowed us to explore our greater potential.

Did we know for sure what life would be like once the moving truck pulled out of the driveway of our new home? Of course not, we were largely facing the unknown. But we were all curious, open to new experiences and exciting possibilities, and we had the courage to take a risk and find out. And we knew deep down that we couldn't make our family's life better without making it different in some way.

Attempting new challenges is undeniably a scary prospect, as it's human nature to fear change, failure, and the unknown. But fear is crippling, an immobilizing emotion that breeds complacency. On the other hand, making a commitment to live your life without regrets is positively empowering. It can inspire in you the courage to take risks. The courage to speak up and speak out. The courage to be different. The courage to live with integrity. The courage to persevere. The courage to forgive. The courage to take responsibility for your life. The courage to fulfill your potential and resist settling for stagnancy and mediocrity.

Unfortunately, there's no recipe for cultivating courage, but the ingredients invariably include inner strength and a robust sense of confidence in yourself and your abilities. It's beneficial to experience the feeling of courage from a young age, and we've purposely tried to foster in you the courage to take measured risks. We've taught you to consider the regret factor, to evaluate risk, to contemplate the worst that can happen, and to have a backup plan if you make a mistake or fail. Having the courage to try something new or challenging far outweighs almost any failed results or mistakes, and enables you to grow as a person. Knowing that you have a strong loving support system in your parents now (and hopefully in your spouses one day) gives you an immeasurable boost of inner strength and self-confidence, helping you to gather the courage to conquer the uncomfortable and the unknown. The more successes you experience by doing things that require courage, the more practiced you will become in taking measured risks.

Not everyone is equipped or willing to take risks, so having the courage to do so can truly set you apart from the masses. Be ready to seize the moment and act on what's important to you when you have the chance. You do yourself an egregious disservice by putting things off until "someday." Don't let opportunities pass that you really want to take; don't let your grand ideas circle the drain; don't let important dreams and goals go unfulfilled. Above all, don't pass up the opportunity to say what's in your heart, for the chance may never come around again. Regretting what you could've done but didn't, prevents you from moving forward. Make a commitment to not spend your life wondering "what if?"—summon the courage to find out.

Our two final stories are quintessential profiles in courage. The first profile features our dear friend and rabbi, Alysa Mendelson Graf, who literally took a leap of faith. Alysa abandoned a law career that she had envisioned since childhood to follow the calling she felt in her heart to become a rabbi. Taking that risk changed her life for the better in every way imaginable, and she wouldn't dream of going back to the original life she had planned for herself. The subject of the other profile is a recognizable name and smiling face to home cooks and Food Network viewers alike. Television personality and cookbook author Ina Garten, a.k.a. the Barefoot Contessa, lives in the town where we spend our summers, and we were delighted to have an introduction from a mutual acquaintance. Ina's success has come from taking increasingly more challenging professional risks, and she explicitly credits her devoted husband, Jeffrey, with providing the encouragement, love, and support she has needed to muster the courage to move forward. Both women have found an often overlooked secret to success. As English novelist George Eliot wrote, "It is never too late to be what you might have been."

Always and forever,
Mama and Dad

ALYSA MENDELSON GRAF

What's the best advice you've ever gotten?

Find your own "dirty little secret"—ask yourself what you really want out of life and go for it.

If you were to receive an award, what would you want it to be for?

Being a good, loving, giving daughter, wife, and mother, and making the people I love feel loved and honored.

Who or what inspires you?

The mountains of Jerusalem and Colorado.

What do you see as the greatest challenge for the next generation of Americans?

Learning to be content with their lot and learning to give back to their community.

What three (famous) people, living or dead, would you invite to your fantasy dinner party?

Grandma Sylvia
Oprah
Barbara Streisand

I f age brings wisdom, maturity brings confidence. And having the confidence to take an honest look within–and the conviction to follow your inner dreams–can change your life's path forever. Just ask Alysa Mendelson Graf.

Growing up in Scarsdale, New York, Alysa had two motivating goals. The first was to be active within the Jewish community, and the second was to attend the University of Pennsylvania. Following in her parents' footsteps, Alysa became involved in activities at her synagogue, Westchester Reform Temple, and instantly found it to be a comfortable haven in which to escape from high school life, where she was constantly teased about her height.

"I stand out a little bit from the crowd," explains Alysa, now in her late 30s. "I don't look like everyone else because I'm so tall. In school, I got made fun of a lot." But the temple was a place where Alysa felt she could shed her insecurities. "At the synagogue, I was accepted and loved for who I was, and that was a great, safe place to be. I was president of my youth group there, and I felt success." The synagogue hired a female assistant rabbi when Alysa was a teen–back when it was much less common to have a woman leading a congregation. Alysa was inspired, and briefly contemplated studying to becoming a rabbi, but dismissed the idea when she saw how the congregation scrutinized the assistant rabbi and her family.

As a high school senior, Alysa also achieved success in her quest to be accepted to Penn. "My dad had gone there, and so in my head, that's what college looked like and I just couldn't imagine going anywhere else," she admits. "My mom always used to ask, 'What's going to happen if you don't get in?' And I would say, 'Well, I'm *going* to get in!' And I did."

So Alysa went off to Penn, following the trajectory that she had set for herself as a young girl, with her sights set next on becoming a lawyer. Despite joining a Jewish sorority at Penn, she made a conscious decision to take a break from active Jewish life during her college years. Penn was everything Alysa had expected, and she adored her studies and college life. "I grew up a lot. I let go of old baggage. I met new people. I learned a lot about myself. And I took the LSATs," says Alysa.

But just before her senior year at Penn, the young woman who had been on a deliberate path since she was a little girl decided that she needed to step off the track for a while and just experience life. She hatched a plan to move out to Colorado for a year after graduating, instead of going straight to law school.

Her parents balked at the proposal. "They freaked out," recalls Alysa. "They said, 'That's a terrible idea! Just go to law school. We've just sent you to this very expensive Ivy League college.'" But Alysa was determined to take a break, and she negotiated a deal with her parents that she would complete her law school applications before leaving for her detour year out west.

Alysa wound up spending a transformative and rejuvenating year in Breckenridge, Colorado, working as a ski lift operator by day and a T-shirt shop clerk by night. With very few Jews to connect with in the area, she felt a palpable absence of Judaism in her life, and grew to realize that her faith was an integral part of her identity. When she moved back to New York the next year to attend law school at Fordham, she welcomed the opportunity to explore more of her Jewish self.

During her undergraduate years, Alysa had worked as a rape crisis counselor in Philadelphia, and the experience inspired her to become a divorce attorney. "I knew I liked working with people in crisis, and I thought matrimonial law was a good marriage—pardon the pun—between legal work and working with people." As she studied law, she interned for two matrimonial judges in the New York City court system, and was excited to embark on her law career.

After graduating and passing the bar, Alysa took a trip abroad, and in her travels she visited a friend who was attending rabbinical school in Israel. She found her friend's career choice intriguing. Alysa remembered with fondness the warmth and security she had always felt while in synagogue, and once again, she felt a tiny spark of desire to become a rabbi. However, once again, she dismissed the idea.

"I thought, 'I just took the bar. I'm ready to go practice. I've been on this path now for quite a long time,'" explains Alysa. "And so I went back and I started my job." But the seed had most certainly been planted.

Back in New York, Alysa joined a small boutique firm and began practicing divorce law. The culmination of many years of planning and hard work, the job was initially satisfying. "I loved what I was doing," shares Alysa. "I loved the work and I loved working with the clients." But as time went on, she found there was one key aspect of being a lawyer that went against her nature. "I hated billing for my time," confesses Alysa. "I hated it. I hated that when somebody was upset, I would have to say, 'I'm really sorry, but this is costing you money to talk to me. I am not your friend. I am not someone that you can come to and cry your eyes out, unless you want to pay me. Do you really want to pay me $75 so I can listen to you cry for 15 minutes?'"

But the euphoria of falling in love can tend to make a miserable job situation much more tolerable. And that's exactly what sustained Alysa for a while. She had met a guy who had swept her off her feet, and the relationship quickly intensified. The couple seemed to be on the fast track toward wedded bliss, and Alysa, 27 at the time, was overjoyed. "I'm thinking, 'I got the job, I got the guy, things are great!'" she recounts.

And then one day, with not a hint of warning, he abruptly broke up with her. "It was a shock," shares Alysa. "I was devastated. I did not see it coming at all. I had come from this very insecure place as a younger person, and I felt like I had built myself up in a good way. But that just knocked the wind out of me completely. It totally knocked the wind out of my sail."

She was shattered. All the insecurities Alysa had felt as a young girl came flooding back. Here, she had thought she was on the path to marriage and a rewarding career, and suddenly she found herself alone, heartbroken, and unhappily employed. She started seeing a therapist, and slowly began to pick up the pieces of her life. "At the end of the day, nobody can do it for you," she concedes. "You have to believe in yourself, and you have to put in the work and be willing to let things go. And that's a hard thing to be able to do."

Eventually, she came to see the breakup in a different light: It ultimately became the invaluable catalyst that made her take an honest look at who she was and where she wanted to be. "I had a career counselor in law school, and something she said has always stayed with me," Alysa discloses. "She said that you have to ask yourself, what is your dirty little secret? What is the thing about yourself that you know needs to feel satisfied?"

Facing a new reality, Alysa looked inward, and finally admitted what deepdown she had probably always known. "When I asked myself where I really wanted to be and what I really wanted to be doing, it was being a rabbi. It wasn't billing for my hours," she admits. "I felt like I was sitting on the sidelines of the best game in town, and I wanted to play. I wanted to be on the field."

So, in 1999, at the age of 28, Alysa let go of her law career, finally listened to her own dreams and wishes, and applied to rabbinical school. "I just started thinking, 'Life is short. You never know what is going to happen. You can think that you have everything you want, and in a minute, it could all be gone.'"

Again, her parents thought she was crazy. "My mom was like, 'You're going to go back to school for five more years?' And I said, 'Yes. Yes I am!'" And this time Alysa was sure of herself. She entered Hebrew Union College with a full heart and a determined mind, and has never looked back. "As a lawyer, you sit in an office in a larger building. I kept feeling boxed in and I didn't want to be boxed in," she reflects. "When you're a rabbi, you're everywhere. You're on the bimah, you're with the children in the community, you're doing all sorts of things. I loved how varied my job and life would be."

Toppling that first domino seemed to be the momentum Alysa needed to achieve the life she wanted. She was ordained in May of 2004, and one week later she married the love of her life, whom she had met while she was a rabbinical student. That July she started her job as associate rabbi at Temple Israel in Westport, Connecticut, where she currently works. She regrets none of the choices she made along the way.

"I think knowing yourself is the most important thing," she emphasizes. "Then you have to listen to yourself. You never know what can happen in this world, and I just didn't want to have any regrets. If I made a mistake, so then I could go back and there was no shame in that. I didn't want to hold myself back; I wanted to try."

Having the courage and conviction to believe in herself empowered Alysa to change her life. "I really do believe the only thing that could stop me is myself. And that's what stops any of us," she says. "It's sometimes hard to believe in yourself, because if you listen to what everyone tells you about yourself, it can be very limiting. But if you stop listening to everyone else and start listening to yourself and you believe in that, then I think that anyone can be unstoppable."

Alysa is grateful for the wake-up call that let her take a second look at her life. "My parents look back now and say, 'We're so glad you trusted your instincts. This is clearly the life choice that you were meant to make.' And it is. And I'm really glad I did it. I love what I do." She continues, "There's not a lot of time for *me* right now, but you know what? I'm living my dreams. And those dreams include a wonderful husband, three delicious little boys, and a great job."

INA GARTEN

What's the best advice you've ever gotten?

Do what you love to do, and you'll be really good at it.

If you were to receive an award, what would you want it to be for?

For empowering people to cook and feel confident cooking, because cooking brings people to the table.

Who or what inspires you?

My husband, Jeffrey.

What do you see as the greatest challenge for the next generation of Americans?

I think one great challenge is dealing with the level of anger in this country. But as for the greatest challenge, I don't think we have a clue what it is—something is going to come along that we haven't yet thought of.

What three (famous) people, living or dead, would you invite to your fantasy dinner party?

My husband, Jeffrey
Julia Child
Eli Zabar & Devon Fredericks

Among the most invaluable and selfless gifts one human being can bestow upon another is unconditional encouragement to pursue their passions and an unwavering belief in their talents. Cookbook author and TV's Barefoot Contessa, Ina Garten, is blessed to have someone special in her life who is truly the loving wind beneath her wings, inspiring her to have the courage to do what she loves to do. That person is her husband, Jeffrey, and he has wholeheartedly believed in Ina since they met when she was just 15 years old.

Meeting Jeffrey was life-changing for Ina, who had grown up in a household in which her parents discouraged her from taking chances. "My mother was very fearful. She couldn't even take the chance on buying a sofa for the living room, she was so fearful of everything," remembers Ina. "I was made to be fearful. Everything that I wanted to do, my mother would say, 'Don't do it. It will turn out badly.' That was the message I got when I was young."

The barrage of negative messages was particularly scarring to Ina, who eventually realized she did not want to live her life constantly feeling demoralized. "I just decided not to live my life that way," she confides. "A positive message is so much more powerful."

Jeffrey was a freshman at Dartmouth College when Ina was introduced to him on a trip to visit her brother, who was also studying at the Ivy League school in New Hampshire. "When I was 15, I decided if I was ever with somebody who was negative, I was just gone," shares Ina. "And here was this guy who was just totally positive about everything–totally."

The couple corresponded for a while. Then they began dating, and married four years later, when Ina was 20. "Jeffrey was in the military," says Ina. "So I finished college, went to business school and he was in graduate school in Washington, in foreign policy. And so I just moved to Washington."

There, Ina landed a job at the National Association of Securities Dealers, leaving after a short time to take a White House position writing nuclear policy papers. "I did that for four years, and I thought, 'This is *so* not what I want to do,'" she says. One day in March of 1978, Ina picked up the business opportunity section in the *New York Times*, and saw an ad for a specialty food store for sale in a place she had never been—the Hamptons—on the eastern end of New York's Long Island. The store was called Barefoot Contessa and it had been operating for about a year.

As Ina explains, "I came home that night and said to Jeffrey, 'I've got to do something else.'" And that's when he said, 'Do what you love to do. Don't worry about making money. If you love doing it, you'll do it well.' And that is as good advice as anybody ever gave anybody."

Ina then told Jeffrey about the food store, and he suggested they go look at it the next day. "Now, Jeffrey says he was humoring me, but I don't think he was," reflects Ina. "I think he really wanted me to find what I wanted to do."

A popular summer community, Westhampton Beach is fairly desolate in March, but Ina met the owner, saw the tiny, 400-square-foot store and instantly knew it was exactly what she was looking for. "I just thought, 'This is just what I want to do,'" remembers Ina. "And so I made her a low offer, thinking, 'I'll go home, I'll negotiate, I'll think about it, we'll decide.'"

She was sitting at her desk the next day when she received a stunning phone call from the store owner, accepting her offer. "I went next door to my boss and said, 'Oh my God, I think I just bought a specialty food store!'" she muses.

According to Ina, it was sheer luck that she happened to spot the opportunity. "It was the first day the lady advertised it, and she told me she was thinking, 'Let's see, I've got a policy wonk from Washington, D.C.–*that's* not going to happen,'" shares Ina. "And then we met and she said she knew immediately it was going to happen."

As Ina had been taught by her father, "Your word is a deal, so I wasn't about to go back on it," she explains. "And so the day before Memorial Day, I found myself owning a specialty food store in Westhampton. I mean, I really jumped off a cliff!"

Ina says that her parents thought she was out of her mind. "My father, who was a physician, couldn't believe his daughter was going from the White House to a grocery store," she divulges, adding, "Remember, the specialty food business was nothing then, so he imagined a grocery store. Even though they came around fast, they did everything possible to discourage me," she remembers.

But Jeffrey encouraged her all the way. "He was out in front going, 'You can do this! If you want to do this, you can do it!'" Ina announces. He also believed in Ina enough to invest in her new endeavor. "In those days, we put every dime we had into this," she reveals. "Jeffrey not only tells me to do it, he invested in it. He's really just extraordinary. He has extraordinary belief in me."

Ina had no experience running a store, let alone any professional culinary training. "In the beginning, I thought it was the stupidest thing I had ever done," she confesses. "I didn't know how to do anything. I had never had an employee. I didn't know how to slice smoked salmon. I didn't know how to tell when the brie was ready. I mean, things you need to know when you're running a specialty food store."

The previous owner agreed to stay on for a month to train Ina, but one day during the second week, she didn't show up. "I was in a panic at 9:00 A.M. when the store opened!" admits Ina. "And the next day, she told me she deliberately didn't come because she knew I could run it, and she didn't think I trusted myself to do it. And of course, it was fine. So she was a very good teacher."

Ina adored her new career, and many years later, it became abundantly clear why it was such a good fit. One of her customers at Barefoot Contessa, a career counselor, shared with Ina the two pieces of advice she gave to clients who were looking to find the right path. The first piece was to think back and remember what you loved doing when you were 11. Says Ina, "Not all these shoulds—I *should* be a lawyer, I *should* be a doctor—but what did you *want* to do." For Ina, that was helping in the kitchen, but as a young girl her mother had directed her to focus on her school-work instead.

The second piece of advice was to design a space that you want to work in. "I want to work in a big space with lots of people that feels like a party, and that's what a specialty food store is," she contends. "The music is cranked up and the coffee is on and there's stuff out to look at and things to taste. It's just fun, and up. My goal was to make it feel like a party, so you just didn't come in when you needed to buy groceries, you came in just because it was fun to be there."

The store thrived, and within a year Ina relocated Barefoot Contessa across the street to larger space. In 1985, she was offered the opportunity to move the store to space in the village of East Hampton, which was being vacated by gourmet retailer Dean & DeLuca. In contrast to Westhampton Beach's summer-only lifestyle, East Hampton is a year-round community. Ina wasn't exactly looking to relocate, but the deal was too good to pass up. "I ended up in East Hampton really not expecting to," she discloses. "But again, Jeffrey encouraged me to do it. He said it would be a great business move. So at every step, he really just gave me the confidence to do it."

She expanded the store in East Hampton and cultivated an admiring clientele that appreciated her delicious, freshly prepared delicacies using locally grown produce. The charming shop became a Hamptons landmark.

By 1996, Ina felt she had hit a wall. "I felt like I wasn't growing," she shares. "I liked having one store, knowing that it was really well run and the food was good—and I had done it. So I thought it was time to do something else." But that "something else" was a mystery to Ina. "A friend of mine actually said, 'Type A people don't figure out what to do next while they're doing something. They have to stop.'" She convinced Ina that the wisest move was to sell the store and do nothing for a while to figure out her next step.

Ina trusted her friend's advice. She sold the operation to Barefoot Contessa's chef and manager, and built an office for herself above the store. "I had no plan. Talk about scary—that's really scary," she concedes. "I sat there for the better part of a year with nothing to do. So one day I was baking a thousand baguettes and running a specialty food store, and the next day I was sitting there copying over my address book. That was the worst year of my life."

Jeffrey, who was Dean of the Yale University School of Management at that time, commuted each week to New Haven, coming home only on weekends, and leaving Ina interminably bored. "I remember one time Jeffrey left for New Haven and I said, 'I have nothing to do this week. I mean like *nothing*," she reports. "And he said, 'Nothing?' I said, 'Well, let me see, I have a manicure on Wednesday, but that's all.' I was really pathetic!"

Over the course of the year, Ina explored a number of business ideas, including the possibility of starting a luxury bus company. But Jeffrey knew that his wife had loved the food business, and he urged her to find a new rewarding challenge within the industry.

Ina thought about it and came up with a glimmer of an idea. "I said, 'Well, people have asked me to write a book, but I wouldn't be very good at that and it wouldn't interest me at all.'" Ina pictured writing books to be a solitary endeavor, and thought the project would be counter to her desire to work in a fun atmosphere with lively people.

Jeffrey encouraged her to give it a shot. "So I thought alright, at least I'll have something to do tomorrow," she confesses. "So I wrote a proposal, and it was accepted immediately by the top cookbook editor in the country. And I thought, 'Oh my God, now I have to write a book!'"

Ina says it was all about wading into the water. "You don't figure out what to do while you're on the side of the pond. You have to get into the pond, splash around, figure out what the pond feels like and then go in some direction–or get the hell out of the pond once you know that it's not the right pond." She continues, "But you can't do it from the sidelines. So even though it's scary thinking about jumping into the pond, that's what I feel like I continually overcome."

The experience of writing a cookbook was nothing like Ina had imagined. "It turned out to be the best thing I've ever done," she reveals. "But I would never have known that from the sidelines." She found the process of writing interesting, and enjoyed developing recipes. She got to work with photographers, food stylists, and prop stylists. She was involved in every detail of the book design, down to the colors and font choices.

But she had no idea how it would be received when it was published. "If you think about writing a cookbook and you ever go to a bookstore and look at all the cookbooks, you think, 'How stupid is that?'" she notes. "I mean, I'm not a professional cook, so it's not like I'm teaching people things. I'm just showing them what I do, just sort of sharing."

At some point along the way, Jeffrey encouraged Ina to pull out all the stops and do the book she wanted with no financial constraints. "We invested about $200,000 in the book. Jeffrey's really taught me to do everything I do as well as I can possibly do it and hold nothing back," offers Ina. "And that was really the success of the book, because I hired a publicist who did a stunningly good job. I hired the most expensive photographer who did a stunningly good job. We literally invested everything we had in it. So that was a good investment!"

The initial printing of *The Barefoot Contessa Cookbook* in 1999 called for 10,000 copies, and to Ina's surprise—not to mention that of her publisher—the book was wildly successful, requiring immediate reprinting. The title sold over 175,000 copies in its first year of release and has remained perennially popular ever since.

Following the acclaim for her first two cookbooks, Ina was approached by the Food Network to host her own television show. The idea was profoundly unappealing to Ina, who turned down repeated proposals. "I thought there was no way I was ever going to move to a TV show," she maintains. "There wasn't anything I thought I could do, or wanted to do, or was interested in doing. I think they thought I was negotiating, but I really meant 'no.'"

Eventually she became aware of a London-based television production company that had done what she considered to be a unique and fresh cooking show, but thought it was futile to mention it to Food Network executives. "But they went to London, found the producers, hired them and called me and said, 'They're coming to East Hampton. Now will you do 13 shows?'"

Ina met with the producer. "I liked her. I thought she got what I was about, which other people hadn't, and I thought, 'Okay, what do I have to lose? I'll do 13 shows.' And that was eight years ago. Again, you've got to wade out into the pool."

Was doing a TV show a scary leap? "Are you kidding?" asks Ina, chuckling. "It's *still* scary! I would say that it's gone from sheer terror to 'just get over yourself and do it.' But it's very scary!" She adds, "What I always say is I jump off a cliff and figure out how to fly on the way down. I'm willing to work through fear—just abject, utter fear."

As popular as the Barefoot Contessa television shows are, Ina's primary passion is still writing her cookbooks, which currently total six. "I have no idea what I'm going to be doing in five years. I don't actually have a dream," she admits. "Hopefully I'll still be writing cookbooks because that's my business. That's what I love to do."

She strongly urges people to pursue their personal passions, and believes that success will accordingly follow. "You don't worry about the money," she stresses. "You never do something for the money, because it's the wrong motivation. You do stuff because you love it. Try it and figure it out. Even if it fails, it's an experience that will fuel what you want to do. Everybody has done something that didn't work out. You don't see it as a fail- ure, you just see it as part of the process," she adds.

Ina is no longer paralyzed by her mother's assertion that try- ing new things would inevitably turn out badly. "It took me a long time to realize taking a risk always turned out really well. I was willing to live with the consequences, and things always turned out better than I could have dreamed."

The little girl who was raised to be afraid of taking chances is beholden to her loving partner in life, Jeffrey, who helped culti- vate in her the courage and confidence to jump off cliffs. "What you don't know about me is I'm deeply insecure," Ina confides. "So having Jeffrey there telling me if I want to do it, I'll be really good at it, is all the difference in the world to me. It's all the dif- ference in the world. I could never, ever, ever, ever have done it without him encouraging me."

EPILOGUE

Dear Boys,

The experience of writing this book has been deeply rewarding and enlightening for both of us. The more we researched and explored the virtues and values we theorized as being the fundamentals of fulfillment, the more critically interrelated and integral they seemed to become. While the letters and profiles were addressed to you, we sincerely hope that the book might inspire others, as well, to seek out real-life role models and mentors as resources, and that it indeed might create a tiny spark for others to pursue a fulfilled life.

We were captivated to have learned more about life and the world from the role models we interviewed than we could ever have imagined, and it was eminently evident that our well-founded admiration for these exceptional people is deeply rooted in the unique combinations of fulfillment qualities each of them possesses. They are abounding in shrewd wisdom, comprehensive experience, voluminous knowledge, and insightful advice, and you should feel comfortable reaching out to them and to the many other luminous resources you are fortunate to count among your circle of family and friends as you navigate life.

Make it your avocation to strive for fulfillment, and savor every cherished step of the journey, always remembering to keep things in perspective. Serve as a proud and shining example to others of how to embody these virtues and values. Surround yourselves with Fulfilled Individuals; listen to them and learn from them. Don't allow the unfulfilled people around you to sap you of your inherent joy and kindness, your respectable integrity and self-confidence, your most soul-stirring dreams and the strength and courage you need to achieve them.

Be grateful for the gift of freedom this nation affords you. Dispiritingly, the message that freedom is a blessing—and not a universal entitlement—seems to become more diluted as generations forget about the heartrending sacrifices their forebears made to come to this land of opportunity. Treasure your good fortune to be living in this country, and hold freedom and opportunity close to your hearts, for it is freedom that empowers you to soar to your loftiest potential and opportunity that enables you to be as exquisitely unique as a snowflake.

The future is at once hopeful and fragile—and you have the profound responsibility and privilege of carrying it in your precious hands.

With love from the bottom of our hearts,
Mama and Dad

P.S.—The eloquent lyrics to one of our favorite songs, "My Wish," by Rascal Flatts, truly capture the essence of a rich and fulfilled life, and we couldn't imagine a more meaningful or poetic way to sign off.

"MY WISH"
by Rascal Flatts

I hope the days come easy and the moments pass slow
And each road leads you where you want to go
And if you're faced with a choice, and you have to choose
I hope you choose the one that means the most to you

And if one door opens to another door closed
I hope you keep on walkin' 'til you find the window
If it's cold outside, show the world the warmth of your smile
But more than anything, more than anything

My wish for you
Is that this life becomes all that you want it to
Your dreams stay big, your worries stay small
You never need to carry more than you can hold

And while you're out there gettin' where you're gettin' to
I hope you know somebody loves you
And wants the same things too
Yeah, this is my wish

I hope you never look back but you never forget
All the ones who love you and the place you left
I hope you always forgive and you never regret
And you help somebody every chance you get

Oh, you'd find God's grace in every mistake
And always give more then you take
But more than anything, yeah more than anything

My wish for you
Is that this life becomes all that you want it to
Your dreams stay big, your worries stay small
You never need to carry more than you can hold

And while you're out there gettin' where you're gettin' to
I hope you know somebody loves you
And wants the same things too
Yeah, this is my wish, yeah yeah

My wish for you
Is that this life becomes all that you want it to
Your dreams stay big, your worries stay small
You never need to carry more than you can hold

And while you're out there gettin' where you're gettin' to
I hope you know somebody loves you
And wants the same things too
Yeah, this is my wish
(My wish for you)

This, this is my wish
(My wish for you)
I hope you know somebody loves you
(My wish for you)
May all your dreams stay big
(My wish for you)

ACKNOWLEDGMENTS

While we wrote *Letters from Home* with our own little angels in mind, there are many other wonderful angels to whom we are deeply grateful for helping to make our vision for this book a reality.

First and foremost, we extend our most sincere thanks and appreciation to the 20 extraordinary men and women who shared their stories with us for the profiles: John Dodig, Eli Zabar, David Cohen, Tim Brabham, Kate Jennings, Matt Jennings, Ellis Waldman, Marucha Andrzejewski, Patrick Ciriello, Mike Nardone, Amy Blustein, Howie Blustein, Mary Lobo, Alberto Lobo, Stefani Phipps, Linda Kortick, Dan Kortick, Meredith Fried, Alysa Mendelson Graf, and Ina Garten. It was truly a privilege to capture their wisdom, their personal thoughts, and in many cases, their heartfelt discoveries and private confessions. Each interview was uniquely enjoyable, and this book would not be the same without the support and cooperation of each of these special people.

We also thank Eileen Oliveira for helping to tell her mother's beautiful story, and Albert Lobo for facilitating the interview with his parents.

With profound gratitude, we are thankful to Devon Fredericks for her warm and enthusiastic support of the project and "making things happen."

Extra-special thanks goes to the ridiculously talented Marcia Ciriello (www.marciaciriellophotography.com)—not only for the magnificent jacket photography, but also for a treasured friendship that dates back to Room 9 at Glen Hills Elementary School and her passionate support of our work on every step of this labor of love.

Sometimes angels appear out of nowhere, and that's precisely what happened one day when we randomly crossed paths on Further Lane in East Hampton with the gracious and selfless Andy Sabin. Through our chance roadside meeting with him, we were connected with a number of individuals who embraced our project, including Dr. Kenneth Offit and Jane Weyl at Memorial Sloan-Kettering Cancer Center, one of the charitable recipients of royalties from *Letters from Home*. We are also thankful to Barbara Pfeiffer from FORCE, another charitable recipient of book royalties, for enthusiastically championing our project from the word "hello."

We are also tremendously thankful to our dear friends Jennifer Freedman and Kristen Haaijer for introducing us to special people in their lives who have generously supported the book.

We give a huge high-five to sand sculptor extraordinaire Andy Gertler, and Matthew Reiser, Ben Reiser, Jake Reiser, and Zack Reiser, who created the glorious sand sculpture on the book jacket, and made every moment of that spectacular day memorable, even when the bone-chilling tide rolled in.

Acknowledgments

Most sincere thanks to artist Noli Novak (www.nolinovak.com) who hand-drew the stunning stipple portraits throughout the book with great skill, care, and incredible attention to detail.

A hearty shout-out to Susan Clegg, Terence Reilly, Leslie Ofer, Nicole Cingiser and Kristen B. I. Cohen for generously and effusively sharing their kind thoughts on one of the individuals we profiled, and to Gabe Fried for being the reigning Spreadsheet King and an all-around outstanding guy.

We are appreciative of our buddy Jason Hopple at The Modern for arranging meeting space for us, and for always having a bright and happy smile.

Many thanks to our team at John Wiley & Sons: Debby Englander for believing in us; Adrianna Johnson for keeping us on track; and Kelly O'Connor for giving us thoughtful feedback, providing invaluable tweaks to the manuscript, and trading excellent cupcake recommendations.

Finally, we are infinitely grateful to so many enthusiastic family members, friends, and even Facebook pals for being our cheerleaders throughout this project and remaining understanding, encouraging, and extraordinarily supportive during our extended stay in Book Land. We feel exceptionally blessed to surround ourselves with such caring people who share in our every joy.

DAVID REISER

What's the best advice you've ever gotten?

Don't listen to people who discourage you or tell you you can't accomplish something. Use it as a challenge instead.

If you were to receive an award, what would you want it to be for?

Raising well-educated, hardworking, fun, happy, goal-driven, nice boys who are respectful and always try their best in whatever they do.

Who or what inspires you?

My wife. She inspires me to be a better person, to focus on only what I can control, to celebrate life, even the small things. I love sharing life with her.

What do you see as the greatest challenge for the next generation of Americans?

To preserve what made this country great and maintain individual freedom.
To differentiate themselves.
To live in a world of peace.

What three (famous) people, living or dead, would you invite to your fantasy dinner party?

Moses
Ronald Reagan
Oprah

David is a Senior Vice President—Wealth Management at MorganStanley SmithBarney, with offices in Westport, Connecticut and Newport, Rhode Island. With over 24 years of professional wealth management experience, he is a Certified Financial Planner™, a Senior Investment Management Consultant, and he serves on MSSB's Consulting Group Advisory Board. David is a graduate of Rensselaer Polytechnic Institute. He holds an MBA from The Lally School of Management & Technology, and an MS from the College for Financial Planning. He is a co-author of *Wealthbuilding: Investment Strategies for Retirement and Estate Planning* (John Wiley & Sons), and has appeared on CNBC, CNN, NBC, ABC, Bloomberg TV and PBS. In his free time, he enjoys fine dining, Broadway theatre, and bodysurfing with his four sons at the beach in Amagansett, New York.

ANDREA REISER

What's the best advice you've ever gotten?

Let go of what you can't change.
Life is too short to live with regrets.
Always take a little sweater with you in case it gets chilly.

If you were to receive an award, what would you want it to be for?

For raising four bright, joyful, gracious, respectful, honorable, grateful boys; and for making people smile.

Who or what inspires you?

My sons, my husband, my mother, my sister, laughing until my face hurts, people who overcome challenges, a fresh box of 64 Crayolas, uncluttered space, a typeface catalog, the Manhattan cityscape twinkling in the night sky, confidence, a playlist of Mozart's works.

What do you see as the greatest challenge for the next generation of Americans?

Prioritizing, managing, processing, and acting on the inconceivable amount information they will be bombarded with and have instant access to.

What three (famous) people, living or dead, would you invite to your fantasy dinner party?

Billy Crystal
Lorne Michaels
Bette Midler

A graduate of Boston University College of Communication, Andrea is an alarm clock, banker, censor, chauffeur, cheerleader, chef, chief justice, chore delegator, coach, concierge, confidante, correctional officer, crossing guard, curfew warden, diplomat, disc jockey, entertainer, fashion stylist, facilities manager, hairdresser, homework advisor, housekeeper, hygiene consultant, Internet safety monitor, inventory manager, juggler, loan officer, lost-and-found attendant, magician, nurse, paramedic, party planner, peacekeeper, personal assistant, purchasing agent, recreation director, referee, reference librarian, relationship specialist, repairperson, shepherd, shipping/receiving agent, snuggler, teacher, transportation coordinator, travel agent, waitress and zookeeper. More simply put, she's a mom with a sense of humor. Her interests include cooking, live music, fine dining, interior decorating, nonfiction reading, digital photography, blogging, musical theater, and root-root-rooting for the Boston Red Sox. In addition, she's on a never-ending quest to create the world's yummiest chocolate chip cookie.